Barbara, an experienced inno... ...eep practical and academic kn... ...of innovation with humour a... ...ns what innovation really is, w... – whether as an individual, part... – can drive meaningful change.

If you want to overcome the ch......nges of innovation and make an impact in your team, department, company, or even your country, this book is for you.

Renate Kratochvil,
Assistant Professor of Strategy, Stockholm School of Economics

Barbara covers the key aspects of innovation in a relatable way, leveraging real-world examples and applying them to 'burning' topics like AI and sustainability. She draws upon her own extensive experience driving innovation for her clients, providing a unique perspective and insights.

Jason Yeoh,
Senior Director Corporate Development at Cognite,
ex-BCG Principal

Barbara Salopek masterfully dissects the multifaceted nature of innovation, offering readers a comprehensive guide that spans individual creativity, team dynamics, and organizational strategy.

Through engaging narratives and actionable insights, she illuminates how to navigate and thrive in today's rapidly evolving business landscape. A must-read for leaders and innovators aiming to transform vision into action.

Scott Parsons,
CEO of Lysara, ex-COO at Unibail-Rodmco-Westfield

I have had the pleasure of following Barbara's work for many years, eagerly anticipating her insights on innovation and strategy development. Now that her book is here, I can confidently say it delivers valuable and thought-provoking content.

I highly recommend it to leaders who are eager to expand their understanding of innovation and ignite strategic transformation.

Aslak Sverdrup,
ex-CEO of Bergen Aquarium and ex-CEO of Bergen Airport.

I am thoroughly impressed with the depth and insight Barbara brings to the subject of innovation. Her exploration of innovation at the individual, group, and organizational levels is both comprehensive and thought-provoking. The challenges she addresses and the practical solutions she offers are highly relevant and applicable to anyone looking to shape the future of your organization.

Barbara's ability to combine practical knowledge with academic expertise shines through, making the book both informative and engaging. I particularly appreciate how she conveys the importance of overcoming obstacles to create lasting change. Her approach is not only insightful but also inspiring, encouraging readers to take action and make a difference in their respective fields.

Sivert Smedsvig,
Partner at Forvis Mazars

Barbara Salopek's book is a testament to her extensive experience and unwavering passion for innovation. Her insights are both profound and practical, making this book an invaluable resource for anyone looking to understand and embrace the power of innovation. Having had the pleasure of working with Barbara, I can personally attest to her professionalism and deep knowledge of the subject.

Barbara's dedication to the field shines through every page, offering readers a unique perspective that is both inspiring and enlightening. Highly recommended!

Montserrat F Telseth,
Regional Director, Norconsult Norway

I highly recommend *Future-Fit Innovation* by Barbara Salopek. This insightful book offers a comprehensive look at the complexities and nuances of innovation within organizations. Drawing on years of practical experience, the author emphasizes that innovation doesn't happen in isolation – it must be nurtured across individual, team, and organizational levels.

The book challenges the common oversimplification of innovation initiatives, showing that true innovation demands cultural openness, leadership engagement, and long-term commitment. Barbara offers deep, experience-based insights into what it really takes to embed innovation into a company's strategy and culture. A must-read for anyone serious about innovation.

Ratko Mutavdzic,
WW Public Sector Government
Industry Advisory Lead @Microsoft EMEA

I had the pleasure of working with Barbara on the CCS 4 Krakow project, where her leadership and expertise in innovation made a significant impact.

This book will be an invaluable resource for anyone looking to build a sustainable innovation culture and implement effective strategies to overcome challenges. Whether you are leading a team, managing a project, or transforming an organization, Barbara's insights will inspire and equip you to make a real difference.

Barbara's approach is both grounded in practical experience and enriched with academic insights, making it highly relevant for today's fast-changing business environment.

Janusz Moskwa,
Director of the Office for European Funds and
International Cooperation, Krakow Communal Holding

Barbara gives meaning back to a buzzword. Her take on a trendy topic actually nails it down into a real talk, comprehensive structure that's immediately employable to everyone from a junior, new hire to a C-suite exec. It's equal parts definitive and inspirational.

After 14 years hearing about nebulous 'innovation' across the tech world, this book left me feeling empowered in a fresh way.

Kathryn Galambos,
Account Executive at Google

A brilliant guide for forward-thinking leaders, Barbara presents her own personal blend of knowledge and experience to redefine innovation across three transformative levels: individual, team, and organizational. With clarity and insight, Barbara uses a combination of academic research and practical experience to empower leaders to unlock creative potential, foster collaborative creativity, and drive sustainable innovation from the inside out and the bottom up.

A must-read for anyone ready to lead creative organizations with vision and build a culture where bold ideas thrive.

Professor Emeritus Eric Arne Lofquist,
BI Norwegian Business School

Barbara Salopek doesn't just write about innovation – she lives it. Her curiosity, resilience, and ability to navigate complex challenges across cultures are reflected on every page of this book. In *Future-Fit Innovation*, she distills years of hands-on experience into accessible insights that speak to the human side of transformation.

From creativity to psychological safety and sustainability, Barbara explores what it truly takes to build environments where innovation can thrive. This book is not only a reflection of her depth of knowledge, but also her generosity in sharing it.

Alexandra Fehling,
General Manager BILD hilft e.V. 'Ein Herz für Kinder'

Future-Fit
Innovation

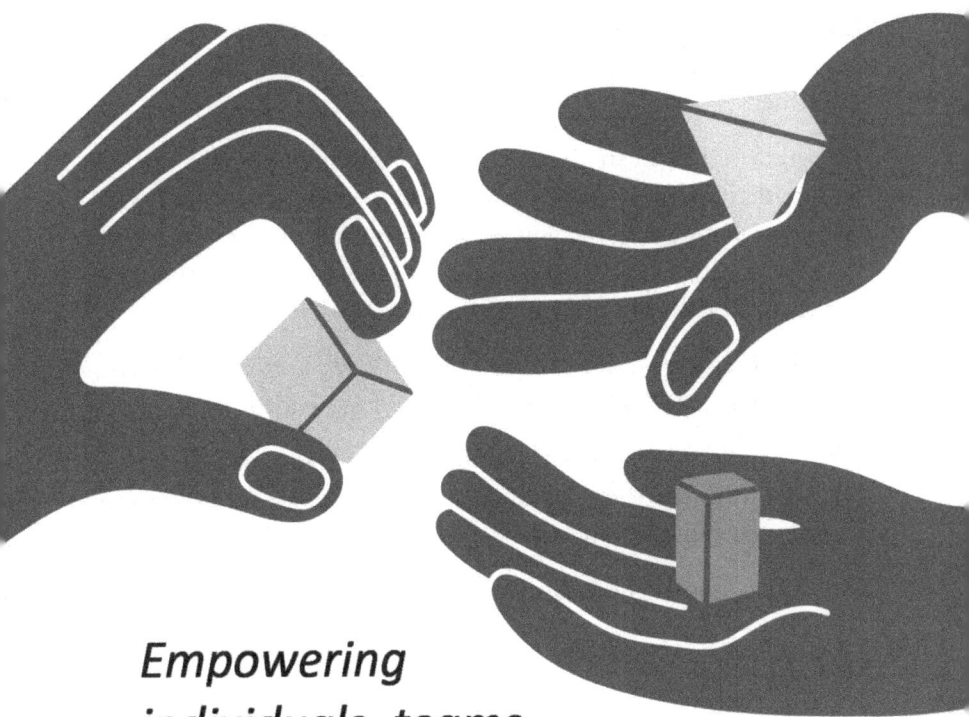

*Empowering
individuals, teams
and organizations
for sustainable growth*

Barbara Salopek

First published in Great Britain by Practical Inspiration Publishing, 2025

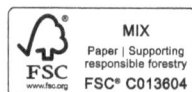

ISBN   978-1-78860-857-2 (paperback)
        978-1-78860-856-5 (hardback)
        978-1-78860-858-9 (epub)

EU GPSR representative: LOGOS EUROPE, 9 rue Nicolas Poussin, LA ROCHELLE 17000, France Contact@logoseurope.eu

Want to bulk-buy copies of this book for your team and colleagues? We can customize the content and co-brand *Future-Fit Innovation* to suit your business's needs.

Please email info@practicalinspiration.com for more details.

Practical Inspiration
Publishing

MIX
Paper | Supporting responsible forestry
FSC
www.fsc.org   FSC® C013604

Dedication

Dragoj mami Božici,

hvala ti na svemu što si nas naučila. Hvala ti za sve usađene norme i vrijednosti koje si nam prenijela.

Ponajviše, hvala ti za svu snagu kojom kročiš kroz život. Ta tvoja snaga je moja vječna inspiracija.

Hvala ti za svu ljubav i brigu koju sada prenosim dalje na svoju djecu.

***

To my dear mother Bozica,

Thank you for everything you've taught us. Thank you for all the values and principles you've instilled in us.

Above all, thank you for the strength with which you walk through life. It is your strength that inspires me endlessly.

Thank you for all the love and care which I now pass on to my own children.

Contents

Foreword

Gaze towards the future and you'll pretty soon get lost in a swirling mist of unpredictability. So much change coming at us from so many directions, in fact the only certain thing in this uncertain world is uncertainty. Which makes innovation an imperative, not an option. If we don't change what we offer the world, and the ways in which we create and deliver whatever those offerings are, there's a good chance we won't be around in that future.

The challenge is not one of whether to innovate, but how? And that brings into play the idea of innovation fitness, of having the right mix of capabilities and agility to ride out the stormy waves we're likely to encounter. So, what does it mean to be fit for innovation? If you take a look at the extensive body of research on the subject (and it is extensive, we've been studying how innovation happens and what we can do about it for over 100 years) we see a pattern. Organizations and the individuals within them – need to be agile, they need ambiguity tolerance, they need ambidexterity, they need anticipation, they need ambition – the list goes on. And that's just the letter 'A'; the reality is that the prescription requires a whole alphabet of capabilities!

The problem is compounded because it's not simply a matter of making a shopping list and then going out to acquire them. We have to learn to deploy them, to rehearse and practice them until they become 'the way we do things around here'. The technical term is 'organizational routines' – the embedded behaviour patterns which allow us to deliver innovation and repeat that trick in an unpredictable world. It's not a simple matter of 'plug and play' using the latest tools and techniques, it's a long-term learning journey.

Which is why this book is important. It highlights the challenge and, drawing on a mixture of research and direct personal experience, tries to give us an integrated view of what's needed for 'innovation fitness' and how we might approach developing it.

A particular strength is the focus on the individual and the psychodynamics of teams and organizations. Too often (and especially in the age of AI) we forget that innovation is a process built on people – their ideas and inspiration, their knowledge and insights – and we need to find ways of understanding and working with it as a human endeavour.

The book is structured to take us on a journey from the individual perspective through teamworking to the organizational level and it brings in a variety of insights and relevant theory. It offers plenty of clues about how mindsets develop and persist and how we can work to overcome them and move ideas forward to create value.

Importantly the book also recognizes that there's more to innovation than progress for its own sake. It needs a sense of purpose, and its operation needs to be reflective, inclusive, and adaptive to ensure what has been called 'responsible innovation'. In particular it explores key themes like the nature of technology, the continuing importance of diversity and the existential challenge we face around sustainability as a key driver of innovation.

Innovation isn't a dilettante hobby but an urgent imperative. It requires a commitment to change and the willingness to develop the capabilities needed to deliver it. Barbara Salopek has exactly the right experience and expertise to offer both a valuable perspective on what those capabilities are and some helpful advice on how to begin the process of developing them.

Prof. Dr., John Bessant, co-author of the textbook
Managing Innovation, and Professor Emeritus of
Innovation and Entrepreneurship at University of Exeter

Introduction

Why I have written this book

I've been working with innovation for more than 20 years. Through all those years, one thing has stood out to me: even experienced professionals can struggle with the basics. I've met many leaders and professionals who use the word 'innovation' regularly, but when asked what it actually means, or how it differs from creativity or invention, the answers often become fuzzy.

Everyone talks about innovation. It's everywhere; in strategies, mission statements, presentations. Yet despite the buzz, there's still a surprising amount of confusion about what innovation really is and how to do it well.

What surprised me even more was how quickly some innovation frameworks become popular. One year, everyone's using one tool. The next year, it's something else. But what I often saw was that even after implementing these 'hot' methods, the overall innovation capability of the organization didn't improve as much as expected. Yes, there might be some progress, but not at the level that matched the hype, or the effort invested. The transformation people hoped for didn't fully materialize.

That got me thinking.

First, I noticed that while everyone talks about frameworks and strategies for successful innovation, hardly anyone talks about the barriers. Every innovation journey includes obstacles. And I believe these have to be addressed with just as much attention as tools, frameworks, and the strategies we apply. As a leader, you need to know what those barriers are, expect them, and be ready to manage them. Most importantly, you need to understand how to turn those barriers into enablers.

Second, there's no magic fix when it comes to innovation. Many books and consultants promise quick results but real innovation doesn't work like that. Like in sports, or any demanding profession, it requires practice, discipline, and commitment over time.

Third, at the core of it all are people. Individuals. Behind every process and framework, it is us, individuals, who make things happen. Individuals who come together to form teams. Teams that operate within organizations. And those organizations, in turn, exist in a wider system, influenced by technology, markets, and society.

So, I wrote this book to bring that complex reality a little closer to the everyday leader or businessperson. My aim is to raise awareness that innovation isn't just about flashy ideas or new tools. It's about understanding people, teams, and systems; and the barriers that often stop us from moving forward.

If we want innovation to work, we need to stop looking for shortcuts. We need to go deeper.

In this book I focus on elements that, from my professional experience, truly are important; things I believe can help close the gap between the urgent need for innovation and the reality of implementing it successfully. Of course, the list can be aways expanded.

My philosophy is to focus on the holistic nature of innovation: embracing the individual, team, and organizational levels because organizations are complex, and made of individuals and groups. It is important to explore how those three work together to create an innovation-enabling culture, and how to identify and overcome the challenges at each level. That is the core of the book.

What you'll find inside

The book is structured into three sections, each exploring a critical layer of innovation: individual, team, and organizational. At each level, I look at both enablers and hidden barriers, because the same things that can drive innovation often hold it back if left unchecked.

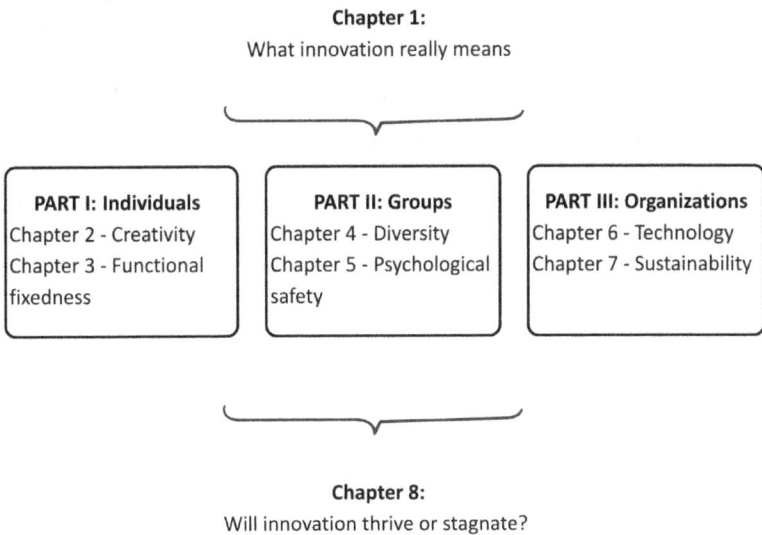

Chapter 1:
What innovation really means

PART I: Individuals	PART II: Groups	PART III: Organizations
Chapter 2 - Creativity	Chapter 4 - Diversity	Chapter 6 - Technology
Chapter 3 - Functional fixedness	Chapter 5 - Psychological safety	Chapter 7 - Sustainability

Chapter 8:
Will innovation thrive or stagnate?

Figure 1: Book framework: Innovation journey from individuals to organizations

Chapter 1: What innovation really means

In Chapter 1, I take a step back and define what innovation actually is and what it isn't. I look at why innovation is so important, not just in theory but in today's real, fast-changing business environment. I also explain where innovation comes from, what enables it, and how organizations can start building the mindset and capacity needed to innovate consistently, not just once. This chapter sets a common understanding so we can move forward together on the same page.

Part I: Individuals

I begin with the individual because every culture of innovation starts with a person.

Chapter 2: Creativity

I unpack the myth that creativity is a gift for the few. I show why everyone has creative potential and how you, as a leader, can unlock it in yourself and others.

Chapter 3: Functional fixedness

This lesser known, but powerful cognitive bias limits how we solve problems. You'll see how even smart teams get stuck, and how to break free using practical strategies.

Part II: Groups

Next, I zoom out to the team level, where the real test of innovation begins.

Chapter 4: Diversity

It's not just about who's in the room. It's about whether different perspectives are heard. I look at how to make diversity a strength in practice, not just on paper.

Chapter 5: Psychological safety

Without safety, diversity can turn into silence. I explore how to create teams where people feel safe to speak up, challenge each other, and take smart risks.

Part III: Organizations

Finally, I explore how the larger system either supports or stifles innovation by looking deeper into two subjects:

Chapter 6: Technology

Emerging tech like AI and digital tools are powerful, but they don't guarantee innovation. This chapter explores the resistance to new technologies and offers insights on how leaders can overcome these barriers to unlock real value.

Chapter 7: Sustainability

More than just an ESG checkbox, sustainability is an important strategic driver and a valuable source of innovation.

Chapter 8: Will innovation thrive or stagnate?

The concluding chapter brings it all together. I look at how innovation plays out across different organizational settings whether you're in a small company or a large one or navigating the uncertainty of a crisis. Most importantly, I share tools and practical guidance to help you begin or continue your innovation journey and lead transformation in a way that fits your unique context.

A practical approach for real leaders

This is a how-to book, but not the kind that overwhelms with theory. You'll find:

- ▶ Clear models and checklists
- ▶ Reflective questions
- ▶ Stories from my own work
- ▶ Tools to use with your team

Each chapter ends with takeaways so you can apply what you've read – right away.

If you are a forward-thinking leader who is responsible for driving growth and transformation within your organization and/or you are passionate about fostering environments that encourage creativity, collaboration, and sustainable growth while addressing significant challenges, such as resistance to change, functional fixedness, and the need to cultivate psychological safety within their teams, then you'll benefit greatly from the approaches shared in this book.

This book is for you, an eager leader, enthusiastic to empower your organization and teams to succeed by aligning innovation with strategic goals.

Want to dive deeper?

I've created additional tools, templates, and resources to help you apply the ideas from this book directly in your workplace.

Scan the QR code or visit: https://vinco.no/future-fit-innovation-resources/

Some materials are exclusively for book readers

Follow the instructions on the webpage to access your bonus content.

Chapter 1
What innovation
really means

Innovation thrives not in isolation, but when
nurtured across multiple organizational levels:
individual, group, and organization

Have you ever found yourself locked in a toilet? Do you remember the moment when you realized that you locked yourself in, and that you will not be able to get out? Remember the panic that hit you at that moment?

A long time ago, I was on a business trip and this happened to me. I was on my way for a morning workout in a hotel gym, but first I needed a quick stop to the toilet before entering the exercising studio, or so I thought. But when I turned the handle to leave, it wouldn't budge. I pushed, pulled, tried again, but the door lock wouldn't move. I realized I locked myself in and my phone was in my hotel room. Suddenly, I was hyper-aware of my surroundings: a tiny, spotless room, pure white tiles, no windows, and silence that felt sharp. At that moment, I recalled: behind this door is a sink where you wash your hands, then the door again, then there was a hallway with loud music and a door at both ends. A chilling thought struck me: 'If I scream, nobody will hear me...' And then, the panic started to rise...

It is often a downturn that has pushed companies panicky into a corner when they first realize: 'Oh no, what now? We need to change something, but what? And how? And where to start?' As a result, suddenly someone suggests: 'Let's innovate. This is going to be our way out!' They heard that there is a tool like design thinking, or value proposition canvas that they could use to innovate. Leadership quickly decides to implement the value proposition canvas. This is now their chosen tool: the one they'll rely on. An innovation manager is appointed to care of the whole 'innovation initiative' and the company will magically transform itself into a successful phoenix rising above the horizon. A brilliant plan.

Little does the freshly appointed innovation manger, and the leaders know that implementing innovation will bring them the same feeling of panic and being lost. We go into a project believing it will be great, we have this great tool that we will be using, but then unknown obstacles face us and we feel trapped, stuck, and panic. How do you get yourself out of this mess? Moreover, how do you manage all this unknown uncertainty and guide it to a successful implementation?

So how do you get out of a market-squeezing situation – not with panic or guesswork, but with clarity, creativity, and a plan that works?

How did I get out of the toilet within five minutes, without anyone's help and without breaking anything? I will come to that in Chapter 3, until then let's focus a bit more on the basics of innovation.

In this chapter, we'll explore the fundamentals of innovation and why it's often misunderstood. Together, we'll look at:

- ▶ What innovation really is and how it differs from creativity and invention.

- ▶ Why companies often get stuck despite using the right tools or processes.

▶ The difference between 'innovativeness' and 'capacity to innovate.'

▶ Real-world examples that show why ideas alone don't create value.

By the end, you'll have a clearer understanding of what innovation truly means and what it takes to turn ideas into outcomes that matter.

I have been working with innovation now for more than two decades. What has been striking me the most was how easily companies think of innovation. Companies often enthusiastically send a few people to a three-day workshop on innovation implementation. Then, they roll out an innovation app to manage the process and just like that, they believe they've become innovative.

The reality is far more complex than that oversimplified process. Even though according to the McKinsey's survey on innovation and commercialization done in 2010 (yes, a while ago now) '84% of surveyed executives said that innovation is extremely or very important to their companies' growth' only 6% of CEOs were satisfied with their innovation performance [1].

Today, 15 years ago since the survey, innovation is still an important topic, a bit shadowed by sustainability, but still very present. Companies are still trying to unlock the stuck doors of innovation. The fact that a simple google search for 'innovation' returns about 2.7 billion results in just 0.40 seconds is a testament to its enduring significance. This vast interest over such a long period, where only a few have succeeded, only reinforces that innovation is not a straightforward process, nor is it easy to implement it successfully.

Innovation is not easy.

Innovation takes time.

Innovation is a long-term dedication.

Defining innovation

What is the difference between innovation, creativity, and invention?

First things first, I often hear people are mixing the terms: innovation, creativity, and invention. Moreover, people ask me: what is innovation Barbara, since everyone says they are doing it? Innovation is probably one of the most abstract business terms. It can be everything and at the same time it seems like it is nothing.

However, over the course of decades, centuries, even hundreds of thousands of years, humanity has evolved and continuously reshaped its environment to make life easier, better, and of higher quality. Today, we have AI (Artificial Intelligence), mobile phones, electricity, self-regulating homes, cars, aeroplanes, vaccines for numerous diseases, microscopes, etc., the list of inventions that have become an integral part of our lives is nearly endless. These inventions, which once seemed extraordinary, or imaginative, became innovations that now seem commonplace, yet they are the result of relentless creativity, problem-solving, and human effort.

Creativity, invention, and innovation – while they are closely related, are not the same and each has a distinct role in the process of bringing new ideas to life. To fully grasp the meaning of innovation, you first need to understand how it differs from creativity and invention.

If you look in a dictionary for the terms: creativity, invention, and innovation, you'll notice a common thread: all three involve the creation of something new, and a concept of an idea. The component of 'a new idea' is common to all three terms, and hence, I assume often a source of confusion and the use the terms as synonyms.

However, each term represents a distinct phase in the process of bringing new ideas to life. Creativity is defined, according to the Cambridge dictionary, as 'the ability to produce original and unusual ideas, or to make something new or imaginative' [2].

Invention is defined as: 'something or the process of creating something that has never been made before' [3]. Unfortunately, the Cambridge dictionary also defines innovation as 'a new idea or method' [4]. All the terms have almost similar definitions. This is very confusing. Innovation and invention are both a result of creativity, but *only ideas and inventions that create value, i.e., are being used, become innovations*. That detail is what separates invention and creativity from innovation. As Thomas Edison once said it: 'The value in an idea lies in the using of it.' That is innovation.

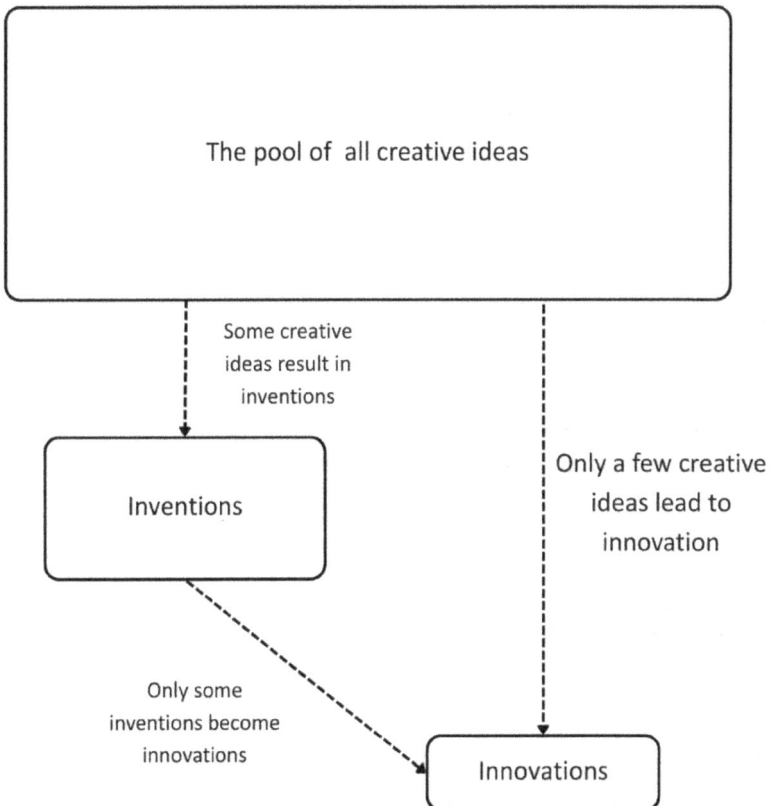

Figure 2: All creative ideas and inventions are sources of innovation, but not all creative ideas and inventions become innovations.
Source: Author.

Let me explain the three concepts using a mousetrap as an example. When thinking about mousetraps, ideas refer to concepts you might have on how to improve or create a more efficient trap. These ideas could range from using different materials to redesigning the mechanics. However, not all ideas turn into inventions. To transform an idea into an invention, you need to refine it into a detailed and functional concept. This involves creating sketches, designs, and even physical prototypes that incorporate the necessary components to make the mousetrap work effectively. For instance, imagine you come up with an idea for a mousetrap that uses a novel sensing mechanism to detect mice. At this stage, it's just a concept. To turn it into an invention, you would need to develop detailed designs and prototypes that demonstrate how this sensing mechanism would function in practice.

How does an invention become an innovation?

Before answering that, did you know that the mousetrap is the most patented item in U.S. history [5]? The U.S. Patent Office has granted over 4,400 mousetrap patents, and it still receives hundreds of patent applications each year, of which about 40 new patents are granted annually [6]. Yet, despite this flood of inventions, only around 20 mousetrap patents make money [6].

One mousetrap, however, stands out above the rest: the Victor Mousetrap. Patented in 1903 under the number 744,379, it was invented by John Mast from Eititz, Pennsylvania [6]. To this day, the Victor Mousetrap, still manufactured by Woodstream Corporation, outsells all other mousetraps combined in the U.S. [6].

So, what distinguishes the Victor Mousetrap from the 4,400 other inventions? While all patented mousetraps are inventions, only the ones that succeed in the marketplace, like the Victor Mousetrap, can be considered true innovations. Its massive commercial success made it one of the most enduring innovations in its field.

Innovation as an outcome

In short, innovation, as an outcome, is a product, service, a process, or a business model, way of thinking, organizing business or a flow, etc... that is both new and useful. If an idea or invention is in use, it creates value, it is innovation. If ideas or inventions are not creating value, they are not useful, they are not innovation! Yes, it is as simple as that.

Another comment I often hear is: 'Barbara, you work with innovation, so you must constantly come up with new ideas.' Coming up with ideas and innovation are not the same thing. One can have a plethora of ideas, but never bring them to life, to use, so they never become innovations. The point of innovation is how to transform an idea or invention into something useful, something that others will see valuable and use.

I know many people patent their ideas, and they think this is it. Except it is not. We saw it clearly on the mouse trap example, patents and ideas rarely become successful products on the market. One thing is to have ideas, and another thing is to bring it to market, making it innovation.

Innovation as a process

Before investing in patenting something you need to have a clear business strategy, to guide your direction, and a strong business case to justify the investment. You need to explore whether this is something that the market is interested in. Innovation, as a process is, exactly that, finding out which ideas have the potential to succeed in the market, why and how we will get there. This is something that Hurley and Hult (1998) [7] call capacity to innovate.

I like very much how Hurley and Hult (1998) [7] introduced two constructs:

▶ innovativeness; and

▶ capacity to innovate.

Innovativeness is an organization's openness to new ideas. How open is your organization to new ideas and concepts? For example, is it allowed in your company to constantly try and explore new things like ChatGPT, DeepSeek, play a bit with Canva, a bit with Figma, etc, in order to see how these can be of use in your company? Or is that not part of our organization's culture at all? Is it immediately not allowed as it pops up on the market or do you need some bureaucratic approval in place to try it? Innovativeness is hence a part of organizational culture that does or does not encourage exploration and experimentation. When I first started teaching at BI Norwegian Business School, we had a meeting about how to teach, and several experiences were shared. One case stood out: a teacher had tried something new, but it didn't work out. The director told us clearly: 'Try different things, if it does not work, try something else, learn from it and try again.' At that moment, I knew I was in the right place: an environment open to new ideas and experimentation. This was a culture high in innovativeness. And over time, this has been confirmed again and again through my experiences with BI colleagues.

Capacity to innovate refers to a company's ability to turn ideas into reality. Does the company have resources, processes, and skills that enable it to successfully develop and implement new products, services, or improvements? This brings us back to the beginning of this chapter and why I decided to write this book. Many companies focus on building their capacity to innovate; more precisely they introduce innovation processes, and they believe that this is what it takes to succeed. They forget completely about innovativeness and whether their organizational culture follows their capacity to innovate.

It should be no surprise that companies primarily focus on capacity to innovate i.e., implementing innovation processes. This is because it is a very concrete and tangible process. There are certain rules that are clear set, understandable, and you can measure whether you have succeeded, i.e., implemented it or not. So, it is not surprising that the focus is on something that is concrete, and easy to understand. Hence, innovativeness and the innovation culture get neglected. Organizational culture is abstract, it is hidden, intangible, and it is much more complex and challenging to manage, to change, to measure the change.

Building a company's innovativeness muscle

Nurturing innovation top-down

In this book, I focus on aspects I believe are essential for developing a company's 'innovativeness muscle.' At the core of this is leadership: fostering, nurturing, and understanding how innovation works. True for any major change within a company, the push for innovation must come from the top.

That is why this book addresses you, a forward-thinking leader, who has the drive to ignite transformation within your team and organization. To enable innovation, you need to understand what holds people back. You must recognize the barriers your team members face and appreciate their contributions as valuable individuals who can drive your collective success.

Building the innovativeness muscle bottom up

While support for innovation must start at the top, the actual 'building' of a company's innovativeness muscle happens from the bottom up. It is the individuals within a company who form teams and shape the overall dynamics of the organization. Everybody has a role to play; no single person can shoulder the entire responsibility for innovation. As a leader, your responsibility is to establish the right conditions that enable the largest number of people to engage in innovation and contribute with their ideas, deployment, and energy.

The 'hero will save us all' trap

Because building innovativeness requires widespread involvement, you must be aware of the 'hero trap.' Organizations often appoint a single innovation manager and hand over all responsibility for the results to them. That person is responsible for a plethora of things, such as:

- ▶ selling the concept within the company;

- ▶ attracting and protecting the funding for the project(s);

- ▶ collaborating with multiple stakeholders in a complex environment;

- ▶ leveraging uncertainty about the outcomes of innovation initiatives and projects;

- ▶ managing expectations;

- ▶ challenging corporate norms and policies to make things happen;

- ▶ managing tensions that will arise in the process;

- ▶ engaging colleagues, teams, departments, motivate;

- ▶ and many more.

In other words, the degree of managerial and leadership responsibilities is simply too complex and demanding for one person to carry it alone. Not only will you need to lead new processes and champion innovative thinking, but ultimately, your efforts will fail without broad participation and shared ownership from everyone else in the company. You can do little if others do not participate.

We humans are raised, and it is deeply integrated in our beliefs, to think in constructs of lone heroes: a single (often male) person that will save the team, a company, or the world. While this narrative is convenient: shifting accountability to one person; innovation seldom works that way. Collective effort, mutual accountability, and a willingness to roll up our sleeves are what truly drive sustaining innovation, and this is bit more demanding than simply assigning all responsibility to one person.

Later in this book, you'll see how organizations like BIR and Sparebanken Norge have moved beyond the hero narrative building cultures where innovation is a shared responsibility, supported across all levels.

As a leader, it is vital to recognize and overcome the 'hero trap' by ensuring innovation is everyone's job, not just one person's burden.

That is why, in this book, I look at innovation through the lens of individuals, teams, and the entire organization and their barriers ensuring that you are empowered with the knowledge and tools to nurture this collective effort effectively rather than relying on a single 'hero' trap.

Innovation is not about a single tool or a single person, it is a collective mindset that flourishes when every level of the organization collaborates and contributes.

Why is innovation important?

Innovation is crucial for any company aiming for longevity and sustainability in the marketplace. Great, but how? It helps businesses stay relevant and meet evolving market demands, while also opening doors to new customer segments, markets, and opportunities for growth. On a broader level, innovation fuels economic expansion, improves quality of life, and promotes sustainable development for all stakeholders. Great, again, but how?

Let's look at this through example of telecommunication and mobile telephony and the use of S-curve theory.

S-curve theory

The S-curve illustrates the typical life cycle of innovation or market adoption: growth begins slowly, speeds up during mass adoption, and eventually plateaus as the market becomes saturated. Constant, long-term innovation lets companies stack new S-curves on top of older ones, maintaining relevance, driving ongoing growth, and ensuring they don't get stuck at a plateau [8].

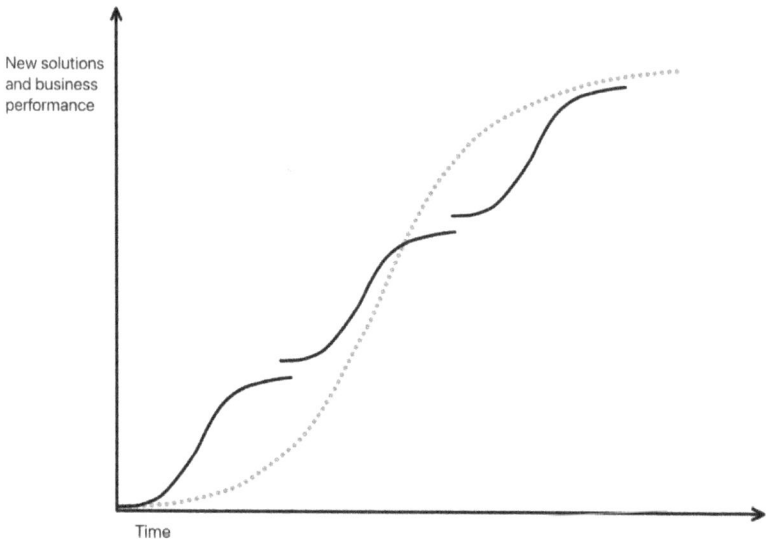

Figure 3: Extending business performance through successive innovations.
Source: Adapted and adjusted from Nunes and Breene (2011).
Illustrated by Mara Jeger.

Mobile telephony: a real-world example

The evolution of telephone services is a perfect illustration of how S-curves work. Initially, the fixed-line telephone defined the first S-curve. When mobile telephony emerged, it created a second wave of growth. Eventually, though, many markets reached well over 100% mobile penetration (meaning people owned more than one mobile device) and growth plateaued.

The industry had reached saturation, so the days of easy revenue were gone. The question became: *What's the next wave?*

How could telecom companies continue growing? Where would they find new sources of growth? And which developments could represent a new S-curve that would sustain their expansion?

Thankfully, data and streaming presented themselves as the next big S-curve. Telecom companies with well-trained innovation muscles, combining openness to new ideas (innovativeness) with the resources and processes to act on those ideas (capacity to innovate), jumped on this opportunity. By leveraging data services and new digital solutions, they found fresh growth avenues and continued to thrive in a rapidly shifting environment.

Innovation is a continuous journey: when one S-curve peaks, the next one must be ready. Organizations that relentlessly explore, experiment, and adapt will consistently find new opportunities to stay relevant and succeed.

It is not enough for an organization to have a single innovation, nor does one become innovative overnight or in the short-term. Of course, you can always get lucky. Innovation is the ongoing lifeblood that keeps companies relevant, adaptive, and primed for growth. By continuously seeking the next S-curve and cultivating both innovativeness and capacity to innovate, organizations can thrive even when markets shift.

Companies that prioritize innovation, such as Apple, Samsung, Procter & Gamble, Sparebanken Norge, VIPPS, BIR, and many more, have established themselves as leaders through their long-term commitment. What sets them apart is their steadfast commitment to maintaining an organization focused on long-term innovation. Central to their success is an innovative strategy intricately connected to their overall business strategy and innovative muscles. These companies have well-defined innovation processes that embrace open innovation, allowing them to tap into external ideas and collaborations. They consistently allocate significant investments in research and development, fostering both radical and incremental innovation. Moreover, they cultivate an innovation-driven culture that encourages risk-taking and skillful handling of challenges. These organizations understand the importance of performance indicators that encompass innovation, with measures and metrics reflecting their commitment to innovation and sustainability throughout their value chain.

Innovation in the current global context

With global economic growth projected to stabilize at 2.7% in 2024, and forecast to hold steady at that pace over 2025–26 period [9], growth remains just above recessionary levels. Slower growth, coupled with post-pandemic slowdowns and rising geopolitical tensions, is creating an increasingly complex environment. In this context, the ability to innovate will be essential for sustained growth and long-term success. Moreover, in a world of constant change, innovation remains the driving force behind not only organizational success but the advancement of industries and societies as a whole. Innovation will be a source of resilience and adaptability.

According to the 2023 BCG Innovation Report, 80% of global executives continue to rank innovation among their top three strategic priorities, with 90% planning to boost investment in this area [10]. This willingness to innovate in the face of uncertainty underscores a fundamental truth: companies that adapt quickly and proactively are the ones best positioned to ride out economic and geopolitical storms. For leaders, this means reevaluating how innovation can bolster not just market share and revenue, but also long-term resilience, sustainability, and overall impact.

With new products and adjacent business models topping the 2023 BCG list of innovation priorities, organizations are recognizing the need to broaden beyond their core offerings. Cost efficiency, cited by 62% of respondents, also underscores the importance of creating value without inflating expenses; a delicate balancing act in volatile markets [10]. These choices aren't just about profit; they reflect a wider movement toward responsible growth and adaptability. Leaders who can align emerging technologies, customer insights, and sustainability principles are more likely to discover untapped opportunities in adjacent markets. This focus positions their teams to create innovative solutions that resonate with today's socially and environmentally conscious consumers.

Sources of innovation

Innovation is fueled by a multitude of sources, each driving creativity, problem-solving, and the development of groundbreaking ideas. True innovation doesn't happen in a vacuum; it arises from a rich interplay between *external* and *internal* drivers, often in unexpected ways.

External vs. internal drivers

Externally, market feedback and open-innovation partnerships, whether with startups, academic institutions, or NGOs, can spark fresh insights and accelerate time-to-market. Monitoring emerging trends and tapping into industry shifts or customer co-creation enable organizations to anticipate and respond to evolving needs.

Internally, employee-driven ideas and intrapreneurship programs are equally potent. By combining deep organizational knowledge with cross-functional collaboration, companies can transform internal inefficiencies or customer pain points into competitive advantages. The key is a culture that welcomes input from all corners, top to bottom and reverse, and a leadership mindset ready to champion and implement new concepts.

Peter Drucker's seven sources of innovation

Peter Drucker (1985) has categorized potential triggers for innovation into distinct groups. These seven sources can come from both outside and inside the organization [11]:

1. Unexpected occurrences: sudden events like natural disasters, financial crises, or technological breakthroughs can disrupt the status quo and spark innovative solutions. Sometimes, even an unexpected success or failure paves the way for invention. For example, in 1945, Percy Spencer at Raytheon noticed a chocolate bar in his pocket had melted due to radar equipment's electromagnetic radiation accidentally leading to the microwave oven [12].

2. Incongruities: discrepancies between reality and expectations expose gaps ripe for innovation. Uber, for instance, addressed the mismatch between traditional taxi limitations and modern customer expectations for convenience and reliability. Features like real-time tracking and cashless payments helped it bridge these gaps and disrupt an entire industry.

3. Process needs: inefficiencies or bottlenecks in existing workflows often reveal opportunities for streamlining or automation. Addressing these challenges can yield transformative gains, particularly when driven by employees closest to the process.

4. Industry and market changes: shifts in regulations, consumer behaviour, or competitive landscapes can prompt organizations to adapt swiftly or risk irrelevance. Leaders who stay vigilant to such changes can proactively launch new products or services often capturing untapped segments.

5. Demographic changes: evolving consumer preferences, new generational cohorts, and other demographic shifts present fertile ground for fresh ideas. Entire business models often emerge to cater to emerging needs or lifestyles. For example, a generation that isn't prioritizing marriage, buying real estate, or having children can significantly impact and reshape markets.

6. Changes in perception: a collective change in values, norms, or beliefs can trigger product or market innovations. The rising demand for ecological goods, for instance, stems from increased consumer concern over GMOs and environmental impact, prompting new, sustainable alternatives.

7. New knowledge: breakthroughs in science, technology, or cross-industry collaborations can spark novel applications and markets. When organizations actively seek and harness new knowledge, they stay ahead of the curve in a rapidly evolving business landscape.

Balancing and integrating sources of innovation

By recognizing these diverse sources, both external (market signals, partnerships, broader trends) and internal (employee insights, process improvements), organizations can maintain a well-rounded and resilient innovation strategy. A balanced approach ensures they neither overlook potential game-changers from the outside nor ignore the latent creativity within their own teams. It also underscores why nurturing both innovativeness (openness to ideas) and capacity to innovate (the processes and resources to act on them) is so critical.

Ultimately, seizing opportunities from unexpected events, spotting incongruities in the market, refining processes, and embracing new knowledge can help companies build innovation-ready sustainable cultures. When leaders encourage experimentation and collaboration across all levels, they create environments where fresh ideas not only surface but also thrive, enabling continued growth and a lasting competitive edge.

Capacity to innovate

Since much of this book centres on strengthening an organization's *innovativeness* muscle, it's equally important to understand *capacity to innovate*; an organization's readiness to transform ideas into tangible outcomes. As discussed earlier, this involves aligning resources, processes, and skills so that new products, services, or improvements can be developed and launched effectively.

Strategy and process go hand in hand

Innovation processes, often encompassing idea generation, evaluation, development, and commercialization, should never start without a clear innovation strategy that supports the broader business goals. Such a strategic orientation helps unify decision-making, ensures resources are allocated wisely, and ultimately drives a sustainable competitive advantage [11].

The reality of failure rates

Even with robust processes, bringing something genuinely new to market carries inherent risk. Commonly cited statistics suggest that 80–95% of new products fail each year. However, the most recent available analysis of this, completed by Castellion and Markham (2013) challenged this and indicated that the actual failure rate is closer to 40% [14]. While this is lower than previously believed, a 40% failure rate is still costly; it means that for every product you launch, nearly one fails.

Moreover, this figure doesn't account for services, processes, or business models areas where intangibility can drive failure rates higher.

Why are failure rates decreasing?

I believe that a key factor behind this more optimistic figure is the growing emphasis on customer-centric frameworks such as Design Thinking, MVP testing, and other iterative approaches. Traditionally, many ideas focus solely on technical features, neglecting the user's real-world context. I constantly experience that a certain percentage of organizations still do that, especially technically based start-ups.

By placing customers at the heart of the innovation process, studying their needs, behaviours, and journeys, these frameworks help teams prototype and test solutions quickly, pivot early, and ensure offerings truly resonate with end users. This moves away from purely technical considerations toward a holistic understanding of the customer. It not only reduces risk but also increases the likelihood of delivering market-ready innovations that succeed.

Such high stakes underscore the importance of well-structured processes that minimize errors, accelerate time to market, and reduce development costs. Organizations that continuously refine both their strategy, capacity to innovate and innovativeness stand a better chance of turning fresh ideas into market-ready offerings ultimately strengthening resilience and competitive edge.

The stage-gate approach and its pitfalls

Different industries and companies tailor their innovation processes, particularly the stages, decision gates, and decision criteria, to match their specific needs. As ideas progress, decision gates, i.e., validation and evaluation points where the idea shall continue its development journey become more tangible and more demanding, including aspects such as development costs, projected profits, potential market share, and performance metrics.

While the stage-gate process is a great driver and decision point it can also be an unintended hindrance to innovation. Clayton Christensen et al. (2008) [15] identify two key drawbacks:

1. Manipulated metrics: project teams may tweak or overstate projections to secure gate approvals even if the opportunity is weak.

2. Assumption of 'right' solutions from the outset: by presuming that the proposed solution is correct, the process often grants premature approval based on overly optimistic data, disregarding the iterative nature of truly innovative projects.

A third drawback that I would like to add is the *fear of saying no*. At critical decision gates, teams can be hesitant to shut down ideas, worried they might discard a potential gem or be left with no projects at all. This reluctance leads to suboptimal decision-making and wasted resources over the long haul.

Conclusion: the human factor

Innovation is inherently dynamic; the initial idea will often be tested, challenged, pivoted, and adapted throughout development. Sometimes, stages can even run in parallel to reduce time and costs while maintaining momentum. As ideas move forward, interdisciplinary teams provide diverse perspectives and expertise, continually refining the concept. The further an idea advances, the more specialized and experienced the *gatekeepers* become signaling the organization's commitment to seeing viable ideas through.

Yet, no process can succeed without the right culture. If employees feel unsafe sharing their ideas or fear being penalized for experimentation, promising concepts fade before they're validated. Openness, psychological safety, and a willingness to learn are the cultural underpinnings that make any innovation process truly effective. When people are encouraged to discuss, test, and even fail, they become more invested in refining and championing their ideas.

By balancing a well-defined strategy and structured process with a supportive, collaborative culture, leaders can harness their organization's full potential for bringing novel ideas to life. This synergy between process and people is vital for building a *future-ready, innovation-fit enterprise*, one that not only generates fresh ideas, but also develops them into successful offerings time and again.

Key takeaways from this chapter

▶ Innovation is not the same as creativity or invention. Only ideas that are used and create value qualify as innovation.

▶ Many companies mistake innovation for tools or workshops, but true innovation is a long-term, organization-wide effort.

▶ Innovativeness reflects openness to new ideas, while capacity to innovate reflects the ability to act on them. Both are essential for success.

▶ Misunderstanding innovation can lead to unrealistic expectations and poor outcomes. A clear, shared understanding is the first step toward meaningful change.

If innovation is the engine that drives transformation, then creativity is the spark that ignites it. Without creativity, there is no innovation – only repetition of what already exists. Yet, many of us hesitate to call ourselves creative, believing it's a gift reserved for a select few. But what if creativity wasn't about talent, but about mindset? What if it could be trained, developed, and nurtured?

This brings us to the next chapter: Creativity. Before we can build innovation-ready organizations, we must first understand how to unlock creative potential; our own and that of our colleagues and teams. Creativity is the foundation of problem-solving, adaptability, and growth. Let's explore what creativity really means, why so many of us think we lack it, and how we can rediscover it to fuel meaningful innovation.

***

For additional tools related to this chapter, visit: vinco.no/future-fit-innovation-resources

PART I

INDIVIDUALS: WHERE INNOVATION BEGINS

Innovation doesn't start with tools, processes, or technology – it starts with people. With individuals. With you.

At its core, innovation is a human endeavour. It begins when one person questions the status quo, spots a possibility others miss, or connects seemingly unrelated ideas in a new way. But for that spark to ignite, the right mindset and conditions must be in place. That's why this first part of the book focuses on the individual level – the foundation upon which all innovation is built.

As a leader, if you want to build a culture of innovation, you must first understand what supports and what blocks creative thinking in individuals. What empowers your people to generate ideas and what holds them back from even trying?

In the next two chapters, I will explore the psychological and cognitive factors that shape individual innovation potential:

▷ Creativity: often misunderstood as a rare artistic talent, creativity is, in fact, a way of thinking available to everyone. I will challenge the myth that creativity is reserved for a few gifted people and show how you, and everyone on your team, can develop creative confidence and apply it across diverse domains.

▷ Functional fixedness: a less visible but equally powerful barrier. This mental bias keeps us stuck in familiar patterns, blind to alternative uses or approaches. It limits how we see problems, tools, and even possibilities. But here's the good news: overcoming this barrier has been proven to ignite innovation. You'll learn how this form of mental rigidity affects problem-solving and how to help yourself and others to break free.

By understanding these two forces, one that enables creative insight, and one that blocks it, you'll gain a deeper appreciation for how individuals fuel innovation. And more importantly, you'll learn how to lead in a way that brings out the best thinking in your people.

Let's begin *where all innovation truly starts: the individual mind.*

Chapter 2
Creativity

'Creativity is not my thing'

For a very, very long time, I felt like creativity was something I wasn't born with. And I have a feeling you might relate to that too.

I grew up in a creative family. My mother, an economist by profession, always had a flair for sewing, design, and fashion. She had a natural eye for combining colours and arranging interiors. I remember her once showing me two fabrics of the same material: one pink, the other purple. She asked, 'Which one is more beautiful?' I stared blankly, confused: 'They both are nice, how is one more nice than the other?' How could I choose between pink and purple when I barely understood what made one 'more beautiful' than the other?

We believe we're not creative

My sister inherited a similar talent. She could sketch effortlessly, adding perspective and depth to every drawing. I remember we had a beautiful fairy tale book, full of princesses and castles. My sister could recreate the images with ease, while I struggled unless I placed paper over the drawings and traced them.

Watching my mother and sister create with ease, I felt like an outsider in my own family. My creative confidence was non existing as I compared myself to them. Because I wasn't like them; gifted in drawing, design, or anything that *looked* creative. I believed I wasn't creative at all. Over time, that belief hardened into a truth I carried with me.

I'm sure you might have similar stories. Maybe someone criticized your drawing or told you that you couldn't sing. Comments like 'That's awful' or 'You have no talent' can be crushing, especially for a child. And that's often how the doors to creativity get closed, as you, like me, start to believe that creativity belongs only to a selected few. This is the moment when a divide is planted in our minds; between the 'geniuses' who are creative, and the rest of us, who are not. And as we get older, we become more self-assured in our belief that we're not creative.

Receiving negative feedback on our creative expression, also often leads to withdrawal. Why should I expose myself to discouragement and judgement? After all, all I want is to be included, accepted, and appreciated by others, at least a little bit.

In this chapter, I will challenge the common belief that creativity is a rare gift and instead explore how it's a skill everyone can develop. This chapter is about understanding:

▶ Why do most people believe they're not creative – and how that belief forms.

▶ What creativity really is, how it shows up in different domains, and why it matters.

▶ The internal and external barriers that block creativity at work.

▶ How personality traits like openness and intellect influence creative potential.

▶ What leaders can do to unlock creativity across their team.

By the end of the chapter, you'll know how to spot and nurture creativity in yourself and others, and how to start creating the conditions where ideas can grow.

The creativity gap

You and I are not alone in this reasoning that creativity belongs to a selected few. In 2012, Adobe conducted a study to determine how people perceive their own creativity [16]. The results showed that only 25% of individuals believed they were creative. The remaining 75% felt they weren't living up to their creative potential [16]. However, there's some good news: creativity since then subsequently gained more attention, and there has been a growing recognition that creativity can be learned. When Adobe repeated the study in 2016 [17], the percentage of people who believed they were creative had risen to 41%.

What does that mean for you as a leader and for your workplace? This means that at least every other colleague or employee of yours has the same belief. And when you ask them to be creative, or to come up with a creative solution, more than every other will think: 'Creativity is not my thing.' This will make them reluctant to contribute, as they believe they do not have the needed talent and will hence be hesitant to accept the task. The request will make them very uncomfortable, and they will be looking for a way out. Very similar outcome you will get them if you tell them to 'think outside of the box' (but more on the 'thinking out of the box' I will get back in the next chapter).

An interesting empirical study conducted by George Land in 1968 [18] sheds light on how creativity *changes* over time. Land developed a creativity test aimed at identifying genius innovators for NASA's engineering and design positions. The test was administered to 1,600 children between the ages of four and five, and astonishingly, 98% of them qualified as having 'genius' levels of creative imagination. However, when Land tested the same group later in life, the results showed a dramatic decline. By age ten, only 32% still qualified as creative geniuses. By age 15, that number had dropped to just 10%, and by adulthood (with an average age of 31), only 2% of the group still qualified.

These findings raise immediate and profound questions: What happens to us as we grow older? Why do we inhibit our creativity so significantly as we age? While I'll explore answers to this question more deeply in the next chapter, let me stay a bit longer on the notion that 'creativity is not my thing.'

We are all creative

We are convinced creativity is an inherent trait we simply don't have. But that's an old-fashioned view. The truth is, you are creative in your own way and, more importantly, creativity is something you can train and develop. The question isn't whether you are creative, but in which fields you are creative, and how you can nurture and strengthen your creativity.

Creativity is not just about drawing, painting, or design; it's a way of thinking, problem-solving, and expressing ourselves in countless ways. And yet, so many of us walk through life convinced we lack it, when in reality, it's something we all possess, waiting to be unlocked.

We have created the world as we know it today, not because of a few exceptional creative individuals, but because entire societies and cultures moved forward, embracing creativity in daily life. We combined everyday creativity with extraordinary discoveries that advanced our systems and improved our world. That's why **creativity is not only an extraordinary phenomenon, but also an everyday aspect of human nature.** The same applies to companies and organizations. Everyone contributes creatively, only fewer of us (these 41% from the Adobe study) are aware of it.

The mistake I made, and I am 100% sure you do as well, is that we are equating creativity solely with artistic talents. We often think,

'If I can't paint, draw, design, sing, act, or play an instrument, then I'm not creative.' That's where I went wrong: I have unconsciously equated creativity with being artistic. Do I ever consider someone who excels at crunching numbers as creative? Probably not. But you will agree with me that there are many creative accountants out there in the world.

Yet if you look at the definition of creativity, it becomes clear that it's not synonymous for art. The dictionary defines creativity as 'the ability to produce original and unusual ideas, or to make something new or imaginative' [2]. Contrary to what I once believed, creativity can manifest in various forms and be expressed in different domains.

So, the next time you tell yourself, 'Creativity is not my thing', pause and reconsider. Creativity isn't just for artists, it's for problem solvers, leaders, strategists, and innovators. And that includes you!

Creativity: the starting point for innovation

Creativity is the foundation of innovation. Every new idea, breakthrough, and solution starts with creative thinking and problem-solving. And the truth is, creativity exists in all of us.

But in order to embrace creativity, I first need to recognize that I have it. I need to understand where my creative strengths lie, how I can nurture them, and how I can develop new creative abilities if I choose to. I need to bring my creativity out into the sunshine, feel comfortable with it, and let it grow. This requires creative confidence: the belief that I am capable of thinking in new ways and contributing ideas that matter [19]. Yet, many of us hesitate to call ourselves creative, which holds us back from engaging in innovation. This chapter is about understanding and changing that mindset.

As a leader, you need to understand what creativity is, how it works, and what influences it, both internally and externally. When you do, you'll be able to help your team to open up, build their creative confidence, and share their ideas without the stomach cramps that come from fear of judgement. The more comfortable they feel, the more freely they will contribute, fueling your company's innovation.

That's why this chapter focuses on creativity. Because creativity begins at the individual level, and innovation starts with people.

Why are creativity and creative confidence important?

Now that we've challenged the myth that creativity is only for a select few, let's look at why it actually matters, both for individuals and for organizations.

Creativity is essential because it enables us to solve problems, see new perspectives, and generate innovative ideas. It helps us refine existing routines, explore entirely new paths, and work more efficiently. Scientific creativity drives knowledge-rich discoveries, artistic creativity enhances our sensory experiences, and everyday creativity, though often overlooked, can improve daily life or provide critical solutions in challenging situations.

In 2016, creativity was ranked as the most important skill for senior marketers and brand editors [20]. It is also highly valued across industries and professions. More than ever, businesses recognize the need for creative individuals who can collaborate and contribute to their organization's innovation efforts.

Given its significance, how does creativity, or the process of being creative, affect us?

If creativity is such a valuable skill, what exactly does it do for us? How does it impact not just individuals but also teams, businesses, and even society as a whole? Let's explore the wide range of benefits creativity brings; personally, professionally, and globally.

The benefits of creativity

Creativity enriches both individuals and organizations in many ways. Richards [21] explored this by asking people to complete the phrase, 'When I am creative, I am...' The responses revealed that creativity helps individuals be:

▶ Dynamic: recognizing and embracing change.

▶ Conscious: staying present and aware of experiences.

▶ Healthy: contributing to overall well-being.

▶ Non-defensive: understanding both conscious and unconscious influences.

▶ Open: welcoming new experiences.

▶ Integrating: appreciating complexity and multiple perspectives.

▶ Actively observing: engaging in deep mental participation.

▶ Caring: guided by compassion and values.

▶ Collaborative: working with others to resolve conflicts and achieve goals.

▶ Explorative: going beyond stereotypes and embracing the unknown.

▶ Developing: contributing to personal and others' growth.

▶ Brave: taking risks and exploring the unknown.

Beyond these personal benefits, creativity also has a broader impact. A study by Forgeard and Kaufman (2006) [8] analyzed scientific research and found that creativity positively influences multiple areas, including:

▶ Job satisfaction: increasing fulfilment and improving business performance.

▶ Business and productivity: enhancing organizational outcomes and competitive advantage.

▶ Education: boosting student performance and learning.

▶ Personal achievement: fostering success in creative fields, academia, and employment.

▶ Social and global progress: driving positive societal, political, and historical change.

▶ Health and well-being: reducing stress, anxiety, and depression while improving mental and physical health.

▶ Problem-solving and cognition: sharpening analytical and creative thinking skills.

▶ Collaboration and communication: strengthening teamwork and interpersonal relationships.

At an individual level, creativity increases self-fulfilment, improves our ability to navigate uncertainty and risk, and supports mental well-being. It enhances brain function and boosts problem-solving abilities.

At an organizational level, creativity drives productivity, improves workplace culture, and optimizes processes. Most importantly, it fuels the development of new ideas and solutions ultimately transforming businesses into more innovative, profitable, and sustainable organizations.

Defining creativity

What is creativity? You might think of it as coming up with something new: an original idea, a fresh solution, or an unexpected perspective. And you'd be right.

Creativity is often defined as the process of generating something that is both **novel and useful** [23]. But doesn't that sound like innovation?

The two are closely linked, but they're not quite the same. **Creativity is about generating ideas. Innovation is about applying them.** As I have explained in the previous chapter, you can have a brilliant creative idea that never turns into something practical. Likewise, you can have an innovation that isn't particularly creative; it might just be an improvement on an existing process.

After all, just because an idea is different or new doesn't necessarily make it creative [24]. And usefulness? Can something be creative if it's new, but not useful?

Usefulness isn't always about practical function, something can be valuable in an intellectual, emotional, or even philosophical way.

Think about art. Painting doesn't serve a functional purpose in the way a tool does. Yet it can move people, provoke thoughts, or create a sense of beauty. That, in itself, makes it meaningful and in turn useful.

But this raises another question: *Useful to whom? In what context? And at what time?* [25]. Creativity is often subjective. What seems pointless to one person might be groundbreaking to another. History is full of ideas that were dismissed at first but later changed the world.

That brings us back to the connection between creativity and innovation. When Monet introduced his unique painting technique, it was an innovation in the art world; a new approach that challenged traditional styles. But each of his individual paintings? Those were acts of creativity, not innovation. Creativity is about the expression of new ideas, while innovation is about their application and impact.

The same distinction applies beyond art. Take the Wright brothers, for example. The idea of human flight had existed for centuries – people imagined it in myths and sketches long before it became reality. But imagining flight was just creativity. It didn't yet have practical application. What made the Wright brothers innovators was that they turned their creative vision into reality. By combining engineering, problem-solving, and relentless experimentation, they transformed an idea into something that worked: a true innovation that changed the world.

This also means that creativity isn't just about having a brilliant idea, it's about convincing others of its value. As Carlsen and colleagues suggest, ideas don't emerge fully formed as both new and useful. Instead, they become creative as they evolve, shaped through collaboration, refinement, and the way they resonate with others.

And as individuals, we don't exist in a vacuum. We are part of teams, organizations, and society as a whole. Our ideas gain meaning, evolve, and take shape through interaction with others, and through innovation processes, influenced by the environments we work in and live in.

But how do we determine whether an idea is truly creative? Not every new idea is useful, and not every unique concept resonates with others. Creativity isn't just about producing something different. Sundararajan and Averill (2018) [26] define three key criteria on how creativity sparks response:

1. Effectiveness: it must successfully meet a challenge.

2. Novelty: it must be unique or different.

3. Authenticity: it must reflect the individual's true perspective.

With the rapid rise of AI, creativity is facing new challenges. How will originality and authenticity be preserved when AI-generated content becomes more prevalent? This is a question leaders will need to grapple with in the years ahead.

In this sense, creativity isn't just about producing something new and useful. It's also deeply personal. It's about how ideas connect with individual perspectives and how they grow through interaction. That's why, as a leader, understanding creativity in all its dimensions is essential. Your role isn't just to encourage innovation, it's to create an environment where creativity can thrive. When you recognize how creativity works, you can better guide and support your employees and colleagues, helping them unlock their full potential.

And that brings us back to a key theme of this chapter: creativity is not an exclusive gift – it's an evolving process that we all take part in.

Domains of creativity

By now, we've established that creativity isn't limited to artistic expression. It takes many forms: scientific discoveries, innovative problem-solving, and the creative ways we handle everyday challenges.

But if creativity can show up in so many areas, how do we make sense of it? How do we categorize the different ways people express creativity?

Creativity exists in multiple domains, each requiring different skills, mindsets, and approaches. Some people innovate in labs, others through storytelling, design, or even how they structure their day. Understanding these domains helps you recognize and nurture creativity, both in yourself and in others.

So, in which domains can creativity be expressed? Or in other words, where does your creativity show up?

The three key domains that are central to this discussion are: **artistic, scientific, and everyday creativity**. But they are by no means exhaustive. Some argue that humour deserves its own category, and creativity can be expressed in countless ways. However, for this book, I will focus on these three.

Artistic creativity

When most people think of creativity, they picture art paintings, music, dance, theater, and literature. But artistic creativity also extends to modern media, including TV shows, films, and even social media content. The rise of platforms like TikTok and Instagram have made artistic expression more accessible, particularly for younger generations, boosting their creative confidence in ways that traditional art forms may not have.

Scientific creativity

There's a common misconception that deep expertise limits creativity – that the more you specialize in a field, the less room there is for original thinking. A businessperson recently told me, 'If you have deep knowledge in a specific field, you cannot be creative'. But the opposite is true! Some of the most groundbreaking scientific discoveries have come from those who knew their fields deeply yet dared to challenge existing ideas.

Scientific creativity is about solving problems, making discoveries, and thinking in new ways within the realm of science [27]. It requires both deep technical knowledge and the ability to think outside the box. Kocabas (1993) identifies four key aspects of scientific creativity [28]:

1. Knowledge: understanding a scientific field deeply.

2. Problem formulation: defining meaningful research questions.

3. Exploring possibilities: expanding the 'problem space' to find solutions.

4. Rigor and methodology: using structured methods to test ideas. Unlike artistic creativity, scientific creativity relies more on precision and systematic exploration, but both forms push boundaries and open new possibilities.

Everyday creativity

Everyday creativity is something we all engage in, often without realizing it. Making lunch with whatever is left in the fridge – that's creativity. So is fixing something with an improvised tool, finding a new route to work, or figuring out how to entertain a child with only what's on hand. These may seem like minor acts, but small creative solutions often lead to major breakthroughs, after all, fire and the wheel started as everyday innovations. Yet, this type of creativity is often:

- underrecognized;
- underdeveloped; and
- under-rewarded.

These constitute what some call the '3 U's' [29]. But just because it isn't always celebrated doesn't mean it isn't valuable. In fact, everyday creativity is often the foundation for larger innovations. Small improvements to products, services, or processes at work often stem from the kind of creativity we use in daily life.

This domain of creativity is just as important as artistic or scientific creativity. Neglecting it means overlooking the very problem-solving, design thinking mindset that drives continuous improvement.

Can creativity transfer across domains?

I used to assume that if someone was creative in one field, usually in the arts, they were naturally creative in other areas too. Maybe you've thought the same. We often admire artists, musicians, or writers and assume their creativity extends effortlessly into problem-solving, science, or business. But is that really the case?

If you're highly creative in one area, say, music or painting, does that mean you'll automatically be creative in science, engineering, or even everyday problem-solving? Not necessarily. Creativity in science or any expert field requires deep knowledge of that domain. Just because someone is a brilliant musician doesn't mean they can instantly apply that same creative ability to physics or medicine.

The same is true in the arts. Being highly skilled at playing the piano isn't just about raw creativity. It also requires years of practice, deep technical knowledge, and refined motor skills. The ability to create something new, whether in music, science, or business, depends on a combination of expertise and creative thinking.

Creative in one domain: is there anything I can transfer to other domains?

Woo et al. found that creativity in one domain does not predict creativity in another [30]. Creativity is often domain-specific, meaning that being highly creative in one field doesn't automatically make you creative in others. Evaluating creativity also depends on context; what's seen as groundbreaking in one field might not be in another.

But does this mean creativity is completely locked within a single field? Not necessarily. Woo et al. distinguish between two types of skills [30]:

1. Domain-relevant skills: the knowledge and technical abilities required for creative work in a specific field, e.g., a scientist needs to understand chemistry to be creative in chemistry.

2. Creativity-relevant skills: more general skills like cognitive/ thinking flexibility, divergent thinking, and curiosity, which can apply across fields.

In other words, the core thinking processes behind creativity, like problem-solving and generating new ideas, can transfer across domains, but expertise in one area doesn't automatically lead to creativity in another.

Think of it this way: a world-class chef and a skilled software engineer are both creative in their own right. But if you swap their roles, their creative abilities won't automatically translate. The chef might struggle with coding, and the engineer might be lost in a kitchen. However, both rely on creative problem-solving, and with time, they could develop creativity in a new domain.

Why does this matter for you as a leader?

First, recognizing the different domains of creativity will help you uncover hidden strengths in your team. You might have employees who don't see themselves as creative until you help them apply their creativity in the right way. When you see where and how creativity shows up in your employees, you can better guide and support them in applying it effectively.

Second, you will free yourself from common creativity myths and misunderstandings. You'll gain a clearer perspective on how creativity truly works, allowing you to foster a more innovative and open-minded workplace.

And third, recognizing these differences will help you bridge the gap between creativity and practical application. You may have highly creative individuals on your team, but their creativity might not immediately apply to the challenges you need them to solve. Your role as a leader is to help them translate their creativity into meaningful contributions by providing the right knowledge, skills, and environment for it to thrive.

Creativity isn't just about raw talent; it's about developing the right knowledge, skills, and environment to apply that talent effectively. As a leader, your job is to identify where creative potential exists and provide the tools, challenges, and opportunities to help it flourish.

So, while being creative in one area doesn't guarantee success in another, the ability to think creatively, adapt, and solve problems can be nurtured, where you, as a leader, can influence the creation of the conditions for growth. So why not take it a step further? When you encourage collaboration between different creative domains, you create space for even more unexpected and ground-breaking ideas.

Barriers to creativity

Have you ever had a great idea but hesitated to share it? Maybe you second-guessed yourself, worried it wasn't 'good enough', or assumed others would dismiss it. If so, you're not alone. One of the biggest obstacles to creativity isn't a lack of ideas, it's the belief that we're not creative in the first place, as I already mentioned.

But beyond self-doubt, creativity is often blocked by both internal and external barriers and recognizing them is the first step toward overcoming them.

Internal barriers

Internal obstacles stem from our own beliefs and mindset. A common example, as I have mentioned, is lack of creative confidence, thinking, 'I'm not creative' or 'This won't work'. Fear of failure, perfectionism, and mental blocks can also stop creativity.

Another internal obstacle is the experience of a *mental block*, where our minds feel paralyzed or blank [29]. Our own beliefs, principles, and past experiences can prevent us from being creative. For example, if we've experienced trauma in the past, something that triggers those memories may lead to a mental block. One of the most common examples is being under pressure to deliver high performance while simultaneously being told to 'think outside the box'. It is very difficult to 'think outside the box' on command; it is not a hamburger that you just order.

Societal perceptions play a significant role too. Creativity is sometimes seen as risky or unconventional, leading individuals to suppress ideas for fear of judgement and for the hope of acceptance.

External barriers

External barriers come from structures, norms, and environments that discourage creative thinking. Organizational culture is a major factor – how often do ideas get dismissed with phrases like, 'We don't have the budget' or 'We've tried this before'? If people feel their ideas aren't valued, they stop sharing them. Additionally, when failure is not openly accepted, people hesitate to propose bold ideas. A risk-averse culture kills innovation before it even starts.

Creativity also thrives on breaking habits, yet we tend to resist change. Consider running on a track in the same direction every day. The moment you switch directions, your brain resists, it feels uncomfortable. The same happens when we challenge routines at work, discomfort can block creativity.

Group settings can also be a barrier. Research by Diehl and Stroebe (1987) found that while group brainstorming generates more ideas, individuals working alone often produce higher-quality ones [31]. People tend to hold back in groups, either to conform or to avoid looking foolish [32]. Social pressure again. This dynamic is known as groupthink; a term first introduced by psychologist Irving Janis (1972). It refers to the tendency for group members to suppress dissenting opinions in order to maintain cohesion and avoid conflict, often at the expense of critical thinking and innovation [32].

A final barrier is myopia – seeing things only in a certain way. The best innovations come from challenging established views. For example, Wales Hospital improved newborn resuscitation by adopting Formula 1 pit stop tactics. Creative breakthroughs often come from looking outside one's industry for inspiration.

To foster creativity, you as a leader must recognize these barriers and create an environment that encourages exploration, failure, and unconventional thinking. After all, the biggest risk to innovation is playing it safe.

How to increase creativity in your team?

To foster creativity in your team, the first step is to recognize that everyone is creative in some way. Encouraging their creativity and avoiding dismissive responses will boost their confidence and make them more willing to share ideas.

Another key to managing creativity effectively is understanding the personality traits that shape creative potential. Let's look into that more closely.

Why are some people more creative than others?

You lead a team of unique individuals. So, what makes some of them naturally 'more creative' than others? While education and environment play a role, research shows that certain personality traits strongly predict creativity.

One of the most important is openness to experience, which is part of the 'Big Five' personality traits framework. These five broad traits, openness to experience, conscientiousness, extraversion, agreeableness, and neuroticism, define key personality dimensions.

Among them, openness is the strongest predictor of creativity [23, 33].

Openness and intellect: the core of creativity

People who are naturally curious, imaginative, and drawn to new experiences are considered high in openness [23, 33]. They question norms, explore unconventional ideas, and embrace abstract thinking making them more likely to engage in artistic, scientific, or everyday creativity [23, 33].

Within openness, researchers distinguish between two sub-components [23, 33]:

1. Openness: associated with artistic creativity, fantasy, and aesthetic appreciation.

2. Intellect: more linked to analytical problem-solving, scientific breakthroughs, and abstract reasoning.

Studies suggest that openness is more predictive of artistic creativity, while intellect is more associated with scientific creativity [23, 33, 30]. This explains why artists, musicians, and writers tend to score higher in openness, while scientists and inventors often lean more toward intellect.

Conclusion: nurturing creative potential around you

Recognizing and developing creativity in your team

Look around your team. Who naturally questions ideas, explores new perspectives, and challenges norms? Instead of seeing these individuals as 'difficult' because they always have a question or suggestion, recognize that they are high in openness and that's a strength. Encourage them to keep exploring.

For those who are lower in openness, you can strategically help them become more comfortable with new experiences:

► Have conversations with them, acknowledge that discomfort with creativity is normal. Help them understand where this hesitation comes from and remind them that creativity exists in everyone.

► Introduce them to new environments. If they rarely engage in artistic or cultural activities, create safe opportunities for exploration. For example, organize a team-building activity at a theatre and discuss the experience afterward. Gently expose them to new perspectives, observe their reactions, and support them as they step outside their comfort zones.

Your role as a leader in fostering creativity

► Communicate often and lead by example. Show that curiosity fuels idea generation, but true creative achievement requires long-term commitment.

► Address both internal and external obstacles that may be limiting creativity in your team.

► Remember: the most creative individuals aren't just those who generate ideas, but those who refine, develop, and apply them over time.

Managing creative individuals requires flexibility. **Highly creative people often resist rigid structures and challenge authority, not out of defiance, but because they see possibilities beyond existing frameworks.** Encourage their intellectual curiosity while providing the right balance of direction and freedom.

Key takeaways from this chapter

▶ Creativity is not a rare talent. It's a skill that can be developed, nurtured, and applied across different domains.

▶ Most people underestimate their creative potential due to early experiences, internal doubts, or misconceptions about what creativity really means.

▶ Creativity shows up in many forms: artistic, scientific, and everyday creativity. Each of them has unique value in the workplace.

▶ Internal barriers like self-doubt and perfectionism, and external ones like rigid cultures or groupthink, often block creative expression.

▶ Leaders play a key role in recognizing creative traits, encouraging exploration, and creating environments that support new ideas.

By taking some of the steps outlined above, you're already laying the foundation for a more creative and innovative team. In fact, this is just the beginning of a concept – psychological safety – I'll explore further in Chapter 5.

But before we get there, let's dive into one of the biggest psychological obstacles to innovation – one that operates at the individual level yet unconsciously spreads through teams and organizations: functional fixedness. This deeply ingrained mindset keeps us from seeing new possibilities, limits creative problem-solving, and stands in the way of true innovation.

***

For additional tools related to this chapter, visit: vinco.no/future-fit-innovation-resources

Chapter 3
Functional fixedness

How did I get myself out of the locked toilet in five minutes, without breaking anything and without anyone's help? No, the door did not magically open suddenly. I had to open it. But to open it I needed to be 'creative' or better yet, I needed to 'think out of the box.'

How did I escape from that locked toilet?

When I realized the key was stuck and I simply couldn't turn it, I felt panic slowly rising through my body, from my legs up. It's very common to freeze up when we encounter a sudden problem. The problem can be an everyday challenge, a work-related issue, a demanding customer or a big environmental problem. Often, we experience that feeling of being stuck. We look around and see no way out.

Innovation often feels like that: we're trying to make a solution work, yet we're struggling to find the way forward. We feel trapped and helpless, unsure how to break free from the limitations in our thinking. And the worst of all I think is when they say to us: 'think out of the box!' If it was so easy, I would already be thinking out of the box and would not be stuck, right? Thinking outside the box means temporarily setting aside what we already know and looking at the problem from a different angle. But that is not so easy. We all experience this mental block. We stay stuck for a while. We struggle to see beyond the obvious. A mental block paralyzes us.

You can always panic!

As I felt the panic building, I managed to stay calm by reasoning with myself: 'Ok, I can always panic. But before that, let me see if there's something I can do to get myself out. If I can't find a solution, then I'll let the panic take over.' I think that giving myself permission to panic later relaxed me and helped me stay calm in that critical moment. I knew I would always have the option of panicking and having that choice was soothing.

Archimedes law of lever

I began scanning the room, thinking, 'Is there at least one thing here that I could somehow use to get myself out?' And then, I saw it: a simple toilet brush. I remembered Archimedes' law of the lever: 'Give me a lever long enough and a fulcrum on which to place it, and I shall move the world.'

Figure 4: Archimedes' law of the lever.
Source: Illustrated by Mara Jeger.

In that moment, I instinctively dismantled the toilet brush in my mind: I broke it down into a stick and a ball. I realized its stick part could be used as a lever to turn the door key.

And just like that, I was out within five minutes, without breaking anything and without anyone's help. I walked out of that door as a proud winner!

In this chapter, we'll dive deeper into:

▶ What functional fixedness really is and why it silently blocks innovation.

▶ How this cognitive bias shows up in everyday work and leadership decisions.

▶ The psychological roots of fixed thinking, including instincts, experience, and loss aversion.

▶ How leaders can identify and dismantle functional fixedness within teams and systems.

▶ A proven technique, the Generic-Parts Technique (GPT), to systematically break free from fixed thinking and unlock new solutions.

By the end, you'll understand how to spot mental rigidity in yourself and your team and how to lead with a mindset that opens doors instead of sticking with the familiar.

Magnus the magician

Similarly, I recently watched a Norwegian TV show called *Nasjonalt Mesterskap i Gjemsel* (National Championship in Hide-and-Seek), where contestants faced a unique challenge: they had to hide in a 4x4 metre open space, which was a garden of a wooden house. The contestants were given a few different objects like chairs, umbrellas, boxes, toys, etc. to aid in their hiding efforts. Watching them puzzle over how to use the objects creatively to conceal themselves was fascinating. Most participants attempted various ways to shield themselves within the small space, working hard to hide with the help of available objects provided. Just like I initially focused only on the traditional way of unlocking a door, the contestants in this competition were fixated on the given objects rather than looking at the bigger picture.

Then, one contestant, Magnus, stepped up and he solved the challenge brilliantly. Rather than relying on the objects scattered around him, he took a different approach. The 4x4 space bordered the wall of the house, which had an entrance door. Magnus simply opened the door and hid behind it. His solution was quick, effective, and flawless. He couldn't be discovered.

Magnus was the only contestant who managed to break free from the functional fixedness of using the assigned objects from the garden to solve the challenge. By thinking beyond the immediate tools given, he found a solution others missed.

Why did Magnus manage to see this solution so easily? Why did all of the other participants struggled to 'think outside of the box'? What allowed Magnus to see the solution so quickly while others struggled? The answer lies in how our brains instinctively limit us, something called functional fixedness.

Discovering functional fixedness

This experience, though seemingly trivial, illustrates a deeper psychological phenomenon that impacts how we solve problems. Magnus' ability to see beyond the given objects mirrors what psychologists have studied for decades: why do we struggle to break free from our assumptions? This is where Karl Duncker's research comes in. What seems like a simple game, or a lucky insight, actually reveals a powerful mental block that affects us all. Karl Duncker, a Gestalt psychologist, was deeply interested in why we get stuck in moments like these and what factors influence this mental block [34]. He defined the term *functional fixedness* to describe the inability to find a solution when we're held in place by our fixed ideas about an object's purpose.

Magnus' solution, how he hid, was a perfect example of how overcoming functional fixedness can lead to the most efficient and innovative solutions.

Candles without light

Duncker is best known for his famous 'candle problem' experiment, which illustrates the functional fixedness concept [34].

In his experiment, Duncker asked participants to fix and light a candle on the wall so that the wax wouldn't drip onto the table or floor below. They were given only a box of matches and a box of thumbtacks to work with.

Most participants struggled with the puzzle until Duncker gave them a subtle hint: he emptied the thumbtacks out of the box. Suddenly, many realized that the box itself could be used as a platform for the candle, which they could tack to the wall [35].

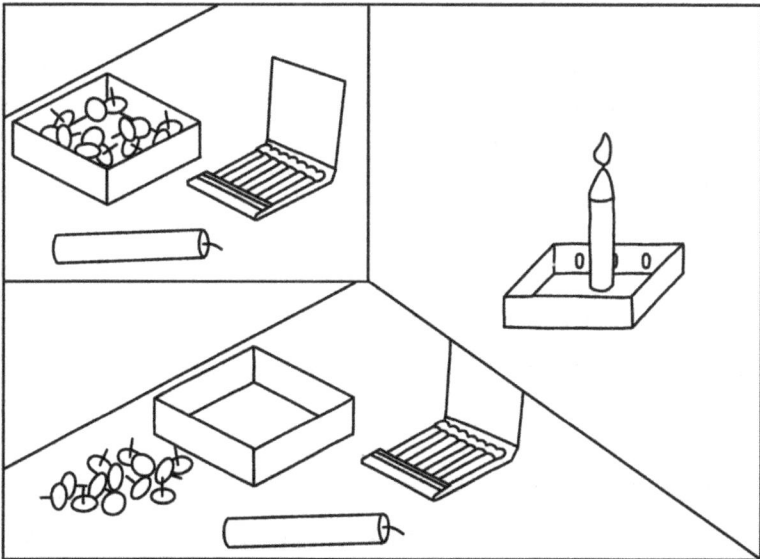

Figure 5: Functional Fixedness in action: Duncker's candle problem.
Source: Adjusted and adapted from Duncker (1945). Illustrated by Mara Jeger.

I often use this example in my workshops, and the results are similar: people find it challenging to solve the puzzle. Just like the candle problem, participants struggled to see the box as more than a container, the hide-and-seek contestants focused only on the objects they were given. Why do we, as knowledgeable adults, often fail to see beyond the obvious to look 'outside the box'?

The answer lies in our acquired experience and knowledge. From an early age, we learn concepts, methods, and systems, developing mental shortcuts that help us make sense of the world. Yet, these same shortcuts can prevent us from seeing alternative uses or innovative solutions.

My favourite example again, the long human quest for flight, is also perfect for explaining functional fixedness. For centuries, humanity tried to mimic the obvious model of birds flapping their wings. We were fixated on birdlike mechanisms, overlooking the role of air resistance, lift, and drag. It wasn't until the early 20th century that the Wright brothers, using a wind tunnel to test and refine their ideas, recognized the importance of these forces. After thousands of years, from the myths of Icarus and Daedalus to endless attempts at winged flight, humanity finally understood that flight didn't require the mechanics of flapping wings but an understanding of aerodynamics.

In this context, our smaller frustrations, whether with a math problem or a tricky home project, seem trivial. But each one is an opportunity to practice breaking free from functional fixedness and seeing possibilities beyond the obvious.

Recognizing functional fixedness in our daily lives is the first step to overcoming it. The next time you feel stuck, ask yourself: am I limiting my thinking to the obvious?

But this isn't just an individual challenge, it's a leadership challenge. **If you, as a leader, can recognize functional fixedness in your own thinking, decisions, and beliefs, you'll be better equipped to identify it in your team and across other organizational levels.** Innovation starts with individuals, but for it to thrive, you must first recognize the obstacles, like functional fixedness, that hold people back. More importantly, you need to help them overcome these barriers. Only when you empower individuals to break free from these mental limitations can they contribute to innovation in a truly meaningful way.

What is functional fixedness?

Now that we understand why recognizing functional fixedness is crucial for leaders, let's take a closer look at what it actually is and how it affects our thinking.

Functional fixedness is a cognitive bias that limits our ability to see novel uses for tools or objects we're already familiar with. Over our lifetime, we acquire knowledge about the world around us and the functions of objects. This understanding of objects and their conventional uses helps us navigate daily life, but it can also hinder us from thinking creatively about alternative uses. This tendency to mentally 'fix' an object's function to its familiar use is what we call *functional fixedness*.

Many argue that the schooling system kills creativity, but that's not entirely true. We learned in the previous chapter that we need deep knowledge in an area to be creative. What the schooling system does, they teach us models, framework, they provide knowledge for us to more efficiently learn about the world and society. As we learn about objects and their functions, we naturally become fixed in our understanding of their use. The schooling system, with its best intentions, indirectly helps us build functional fixedness. Functional fixedness is not a bad thing. It is good and required for us to survive. Imagine that you need to learn the use of a chair every day when you choose to sit on it? Or what a car is for? It is much more efficient, and evolutionary beneficial, once learned, to know these things and not to use our energy everyday to discover it anew.

While this efficiency is useful, it also comes at a cost: we often stop questioning whether an object, behaviour, or tool could be used in new ways. As we learn the functions of things and frameworks, we forget to think about them beyond their intended purpose. We forget to consider new applications for existing objects, behaviours, or tools. That is functional fixedness; 'a disability to use familiar objects in novel ways' [36].

While functional fixedness helps us navigate daily life efficiently, it also limits our ability to innovate. When faced with a challenge, we instinctively rely on what we already know [37]. But if that knowledge doesn't lead to a solution, we risk getting stuck in a mental block – unsure of what to try next [37]. To foster innovation, we must first recognize this cognitive limitation and learn how to break free from it.

When and how do we get 'infected' by functional fixedness?

To better understand how to overcome functional fixedness, we first need to explore when and how it takes root in our thinking.

Research shows that functional fixedness starts to appear in humans around the age of six [38] and intensifies as we grow, with older children showing greater fixedness than younger ones [39, 40 cited in 37]. This pattern mirrors the results of Land's creativity test, which demonstrated how creative potential diminishes with age, suggesting that as functional fixedness strengthens, creativity tends to weaken.

This flexibility in young age is likely due to children's limited experience with each object, meaning that the mental associations they form are not yet deeply ingrained. As experience with specific functions of objects becomes more firmly rooted, it restricts our flexibility in seeing alternative uses [41]. Interestingly, how we learn an object's function, whether through a video, picture, or real-life experience, does not affect whether we develop functional fixedness. No matter how we learn, we still form fixed associations with objects [37]. When solving a problem, we are more likely to break free from functional fixedness if we see it visually rather than just hearing about it. Perhaps that's why I instinctively sketch problems when I hear them; it helps me see the structure more clearly. Research shows that images and videos help reduce fixed thinking more effectively than audio alone [42]. So, do sketch and draw when you get blocked.

Functional fixedness isn't unique to humans. Studies show that chimpanzees develop it as early as age four, and evidence suggests it may also affect elephants and certain tool-using species like birds [38].

However, in both humans and animals, experience and repetition shape how we approach challenges [41]. While this helps us navigate familiar situations efficiently, it can also make it difficult to break free from functional fixedness when we need to think in new ways [41].

It's not just in our heads – objects influence functional fixedness too

While we've explored how functional fixedness develops in our minds, research shows that some of it is also influenced by the objects themselves [43]. A study by Kroneisen et al. (2020) revealed that certain objects are more adaptable to new uses, while others have limited flexibility [43].

In other words, some objects are low in functional fixedness, allowing for more creative use, like a table, while others are high in functional fixedness and restrict novel applications, e.g., a calculator.

How we describe an object influences how we think about its potential [42]. If we focus on its function, we limit ourselves to similar uses. But when we focus on its shape or material, new possibilities emerge. This is exactly what Kroneisen et al. (2020) explored in their survival scenario experiment.

Think that it is a matter of a survival

In Kroneisen et al. experiment, participants were instructed to imagine themselves stranded in a foreign grassland, vulnerable to predators and without provisions or shelter [43]. They were given various objects to use for survival and then asked to evaluate each item's relevance in this scenario.

In this scenario, participants had to evaluate not only the typical function of each object but also its potential in new ways. They mentally visualized using objects based on their properties, such as shape, material, and stability, rather than their standard purpose [43]. To come up with these innovative functions, they recalled various object properties from long-term memory and mentally visualized using each item in a new context [43]. For example, a spoon could be used for eating, digging, or even conducting electricity.

This experiment offered two main conclusions [43]:

1. survival scenarios encourage innovative thinking; and

2. certain objects are more adaptable to novel uses.

Survival scenarios encourage innovative thinking

When faced with a survival situation, we are more inclined to think outside the box and consider unconventional uses for objects [43].

Think back to when I was locked in the toilet. In that moment, I wasn't just solving a problem – I was experiencing a small-scale survival scenario. When we face urgent challenges, we instinctively push past functional fixedness to find solutions.

Certain objects are more adaptable to novel uses

Some objects naturally lend themselves to creative repurposing, while others are harder to reimagine in new ways. This means that functional fixedness isn't just about how we think – it's also about the objects themselves.

A fork, for example, has many possible uses: it can be used for eating, digging, combing hair, scratching your back, or constructing something. A toaster, on the other hand, has a highly specific function and is far harder to repurpose.

A study by Kroneisen et al. (2020) found that participants were better at recalling objects that were low in functional fixedness – like a spoon – because their potential uses were more varied. Objects with greater relevance to a situation were also easier to remember, suggesting that our brains prioritize tools with broader applications [43].

Why does this matter for leaders and innovation?

Understanding that some objects, systems, or even business processes are naturally more 'fixed' than others is crucial for leaders driving innovation. Instead of forcing creativity, recognize when the structure itself is limiting new ideas. By recognizing that the difficulty in coming up with ideas can also be due to the object itself, not just your own creativity, you can take a more strategic approach to brainstorming and problem-solving.

The key is to shift focus from function to properties, encouraging yourself and your team to **analyze objects, not by what they do, but by their shape, material, or components.** This shift can unlock new creative possibilities and help your team break through rigid thinking.

The best innovators don't just find new ideas, they redefine what's possible.

How experience, instincts, and loss aversion trap us in fixed thinking

Why do we sometimes struggle to let go of old ideas, even when they no longer serve us? The answer may lie in functional fixedness, not just in how we use objects, but also in how we think, feel, and make decisions. Our past experiences, gut feelings, and fear of loss may all contribute to this mental rigidity, shaping our choices in ways we don't always realize.

How experience shapes functional fixedness

No matter how we learn about an object, whether through a direct use when we actively use a tool, or through passive exposure watching someone use it or seeing it in a picture, functional fixedness still develops [37, 38, 44, 41]. **Simply knowing an objects common use makes it harder to imagine alternative possibilities.**

For example, if someone is shown a tool and is explicitly told its primary function right before using it, they will have more difficulty repurposing it for creative problem-solving [37, 45, 46].

Functional fixedness doesn't just limit how we use objects; it also shapes our imagination and problem-solving. Take alien life, for example. When asked to picture an extraterrestrial being, most people imagine something Earth-like, even though life could evolve in completely different ways. I love how Neil deGrasse Tyson introduces the idea of extraterrestrial life forms that might be based on photosynthesis rather than meat-based biology [47].

Just as we default to familiar ideas in biology, we do the same in business, leadership, and innovation, limiting our ability to see new possibilities. And as a leader, this bias matters. It may even explain why top leadership positions often go to the same types of candidates because breaking through fixed assumptions about what a leader 'should' look like is difficult. I'll explore this further in the diversity chapter (Chapter 4), where we look at how fixed assumptions about leadership and 'typical' users can limit who contributes, how, and who we design solutions for, ultimately narrowing innovation itself.

Gut feeling: A hidden form of functional fixedness

Functional fixedness doesn't just affect how we see objects; it also shapes our instincts and gut feelings. Our gut feeling is built on past experiences, meaning that when we encounter a familiar situation, we assume the same rules apply. However, just because something *feels* familiar (like déjà vu) doesn't mean the outcome will be the same.

Imagine flipping a coin ten times and getting heads eight times. You might feel as if you can predict the next flip, but, in reality, each toss is completely independent. Our **gut feeling tricks us into seeing patterns that don't exist, reinforcing mental rigidity.** This unconscious rigidity can be just as limiting as functional fixedness with objects.

Why we get stuck: ownership, loss aversion, and fixed thinking

Economic theory shows that people feel losses more intensely than equivalent gains and tend to overvalue what they own; a bias known as the endowment effect. Functional fixedness and loss aversion share a common problem: we fixate on what we already have, making it harder to consider alternatives.

Behavioural economist Richard Thaler demonstrated this effect with a simple experiment: if given a coffee mug as a gift, most people would refuse to trade it for $10 even if they wouldn't have paid $10 for it in the first place. The pain of losing the mug outweighed the logic of an equal exchange. This same attachment to what we own applies to ideas, strategies, projects, and even outdated business models we do not want to let go.

Research by Ledgerwood and Boydstun (2014) confirms that people are more likely to 'stick' i.e., stay fixed to losses than embrace gains, making them resistant to change. In their study on financial decision-making, participants were asked to either keep or sell assets that had gained or lost value [48]. Surprisingly, most were reluctant to sell losing assets, even when it would have been the smarter financial move. In this way, loss aversion, rooted in functional fixedness, causes individuals to prioritize avoiding losses over making rational, beneficial choices [48].

Loss aversion doesn't just affect investments, it influences many aspects of decision-making, often reinforcing functional fixedness and leading to choices that go against our best interests. Here are a few common examples:

▶ Risky behaviours: people sometimes take greater risks to avoid losses rather than to achieve gains. For example, someone might accept a dangerous job to avoid unemployment, even if it carries a higher risk of injury.

▶ Negotiations: loss aversion can lead individuals to make unnecessary concessions just to avoid perceived losses. In salary negotiations, for instance, an employee might accept a modest offer rather than negotiating for more, fearing they might lose the offer altogether or damage their relationship with their employer, even when asking for a better package would be reasonable.

▶ Consumer behaviour and pricing: marketers leverage loss aversion through discounts and time-sensitive deals, making consumers feel they must act quickly to avoid missing out. This urgency often overrides rational decision-making.

As a leader, recognizing that past experiences, gut feelings, and loss aversion, are all forms of functional fixedness is a game-changer. It allows you to step back, challenge outdated strategies, and adapt more quickly to change, turning mental flexibility into a competitive advantage.

Functional fixedness is a killer of innovation

If there's one thing that kills innovation, it's functional fixedness. It locks us into the familiar, preventing us from seeing new possibilities. In organizations, this mental block slows progress, limits problem-solving, and stifles groundbreaking ideas before they even take shape.

It limits creativity and narrows the scope of problem-solving

When people are constrained by functional fixedness, they struggle to think creatively and explore innovative solutions. They tend to rely on the most common or familiar uses of an object, limiting their ability to see new possibilities. For instance, when designing modern workspaces, companies might overlook unconventional elements, like using whiteboard walls instead of traditional boards or repurposing outdoor spaces for creative brainstorming. These innovations only emerge when we break away from default assumptions about function.

As seen in the history of flight, focusing only on familiar methods delays progress. The same applies to leadership and decision-making. When leaders approach challenges with fixed assumptions, they risk missing out on novel solutions. Choosing leaders who only resemble ourselves restricts divergent thinking and reinforces familiar patterns, limiting the range of ideas that surface. The key to fostering innovation is not just encouraging 'creative thinking', but also deliberately composing and training teams to challenge existing ideas and question whether the tools, processes, and strategies they rely on can be repurposed in new ways.

Slows down the pace of innovation

Functional fixedness can slow the pace of innovation, preventing organizations from staying ahead of competitors. For example, a company that clings to outdated technology or methods may miss opportunities to adopt innovative solutions that could set them apart. For example, Nokia's reluctance to shift from hardware-focused phones to software-driven smartphones, and Kodak's failure to embrace digital photography, left both companies behind. By clinging to outdated models, they missed the innovations that reshaped their industries.

Reduces the diversity of solutions

By using familiar solutions when problem-solving, or by composing teams where everyone thinks alike, functional fixedness reduces the diversity of ideas. This lack of variety can hinder innovation and lead to repeated, existing solutions. For example, early radios and televisions followed a fixed design for decades, with both devices confined to bulky, box-like shapes. It wasn't until designers began to rethink these devices, viewing them as potential art pieces or space-saving appliances, that we saw the emergence of sleek, wall-mounted TVs and portable radios. By breaking away from traditional designs, companies opened up new possibilities, appealing to consumers' desire for aesthetics and functionality.

Breaking free from functional fixedness: what chimps can teach us about innovation

Peanuts and chimpanzees

What if intelligence alone isn't the key to innovation, but rather, the ability to see beyond the obvious? A fascinating experiment with chimpanzees demonstrates just how powerful functional fixedness can be and how overcoming it can unlock creative breakthroughs.

Hanus (2011) developed the *floating peanuts task*, a cognitive psychology experiment designed to measure functional fixedness on chimpanzees [38].

In the experiment, a peanut floated at the bottom of a transparent, narrow tube; too deep for the chimpanzees to reach with their hands. To succeed, they had to find another way to bring the peanuts within reach.

The challenge was that chimpanzees needed to figure out how to get the peanuts out of the tube without using their hands directly. Some chimpanzees spontaneously figured out the solutions.

Others did not. Chimpanzees that were stuck in functional fixedness kept trying to use their hands, failing repeatedly. But those that overcame it found a breakthrough: collecting water in their mouths and spitting it into the tube to float the peanut to the top [38].

Results show that individuals affected by functional fixedness are less likely to find innovative solutions compared to those who overcome this cognitive bias [38]. This highlights how functional fixedness restricts our ability to think creatively, and limits the range of solutions we consider, ultimately impacting our ability to innovate.

This experiment revealed two key insights into how we overcome functional fixedness, insights that apply to both problem-solving and leadership [38]:

1. A sudden discovery of a new solution that works might appear after many unsuccessful attempts.

2. Once a chimpanzee found a working solution, it stuck with it instead of reverting to failed attempts.

This highlights a crucial aspect of innovation – when we break free from fixed thinking, we open the door to new repeatable, scalable success. This experiment confirmed again that overcoming mental blocks and functional fixedness is key to innovation, whether in animals or humans.

This experiment isn't just about chimpanzees, it's about us. In business and leadership, we often get stuck trying the same failing approaches, assuming no other options exist. But by challenging functional fixedness, we can train ourselves and our teams to break through mental barriers and drive real innovation. How? This is the topic of the next section.

How to break free from functional fixedness – deliberately

What if you could systematically train yourself, and your team, to break through mental barriers? Instead of waiting for inspiration to strike, there's a proven way to overcome functional fixedness and spark innovation.

McCaffrey (2012) discovered that one thing separates groundbreaking innovations from ideas that never take off: the ability to break free from functional fixedness [49]. But what if we could apply this process intentionally, rather than wait for a lucky breakthrough?

McCaffrey (2012) introduced the Generic-Parts Technique (GPT), a framework that helps innovators break down existing solutions and repurpose overlooked features in new ways. Research also found that subjects using this method solved on average 67% more problems than a control group [49]. GPT works in two steps [49]:

1. Break an object into its smaller parts to uncover overlooked features.

2. Use one of these features as the foundation for a new solution.

This approach has been used in one of the most iconic examples of contemporary innovation: the iPhone.

Before the iPhone, mobile phones were built around keypads – because making calls was their primary function. Apple flipped this thinking, redefining the phone's core purpose as a touchscreen device and putting the screen in the centre. This shift not only revolutionized mobile technology but changed how we interact with the digital world.

Similar breakthroughs can be seen in the development of aeroplanes, where humans had to move beyond imitating birds' wings, and in shift from fixed-line to mobile telephony. Each of these innovations required breaking free from old assumptions, something we can do more effectively with structured techniques like GPT.

While functional fixedness is a deeply ingrained cognitive bias, the GPT tool provides a structured way to break free from these mental constraints. Our ability to overcome these blocks and think creatively is often what allows us to tackle challenges, big or small.

How can you apply the Generic-Parts Technique (GPT) in your own work?

Instead of struggling to 'think outside the box', you can systematically break down an object or process into its essential components and discover new possibilities.

Here are four key questions to help guide you through this method:

1. What are the different components of this object/process, and do any of them have hidden functions? (Aligns with GPT's idea of breaking things into smaller parts.)

2. If I describe this object/process based only on its physical properties (not its function), what new uses can I imagine? (Encourages thinking beyond function.)

3. If I couldn't use this object the way it was intended, how else could I use it? (Encourages breaking away from functional fixedness.)

4. What problem would I solve with this object if I had no constraints? (Encourages radical repurposing.)

These questions naturally encourage unconventional thinking without the pressure of forcing yourself to 'think outside the box'. By focusing on exploration rather than immediate solutions, you create a space where innovation can emerge more freely.

Conclusion: leading beyond fixed thinking

This chapter has demonstrated how functional fixedness is one of the biggest barriers to innovation and creative problem-solving, not just at an individual level, but across teams and organizations.

We've seen how it shows up in our daily thinking, in the tools and objects around us, and in the decisions we leaders make. Whether it's a locked door, a workplace challenge, or a long-standing industry assumption, breaking free from fixed thinking is what allows real innovation to emerge.

As a forward-thinking leader, your role is not just to overcome your own functional fixedness, but to help your team do the same. That means questioning assumptions, creating space for unconventional thinking, and building an environment where innovation can truly thrive.

So, what can you do next?

Next time you or your team feel stuck, ask yourself:

▶ What assumptions am I making about this problem?

▶ Am I focusing too much on how things 'should' be done?

▶ If I had to solve this problem with no constraints, what would I try?

▶ How can I help my team break free from rigid thinking?

Key takeaways from this chapter

▶ Functional fixedness is a bias that limits creativity by making us see objects, processes, or ideas only in their usual roles.

▶ This bias is shaped by experience, instincts, and loss aversion and it affects not only individuals, but also teams, decisions, and leadership behaviour.

▶ Breaking free from fixed thinking is essential for innovation and problem-solving, especially in fast-changing environments.

▶ The Generic-Parts Technique (GPT) provides a practical, repeatable method to dismantle fixed assumptions and generate new solutions.

▶ Leaders who recognize and challenge functional fixedness in themselves and their teams create space for more adaptive, resourceful, and innovative thinking.

Innovation doesn't just come from new technology – it comes from rethinking what's already in front of us. By recognizing where functional fixedness exists and using tools like the Generic-Parts Technique, you can train yourself and your organization to approach challenges with fresh eyes, unlock creativity, and lead transformation.

Functional fixedness is everywhere. But now, you have the tools to overcome it. The question is: what will you do differently, starting today?

***

For additional tools related to this chapter, visit: vinco.no/future-fit-innovation-resources

PART II

GROUPS: THE NEXT LEVEL OF INNOVATION

In the first part of this book, we focused on individuals. Why? Because innovation starts with people – how they think, perceive challenges, and overcome barriers to creativity. But individuals don't exist in a vacuum. They come together to form groups, and groups shape organizations. These three levels – individual, group, and organization – each have unique obstacles to innovation.

As a leader, understanding the barriers individuals face is crucial. We explored creativity and the common misconception that it's limited to artistic talent. In reality, everyone is creative, just in different ways. We also tackled functional fixedness, the mental bias that locks us into seeing objects or problems in a fixed way, limiting our ability to think outside the box. Through tools like

Generic Parts Technique (GPT), we saw how breaking down assumptions can unlock new possibilities.

Recognizing these barriers at the individual level helps you, as a leader, navigate and support your people more effectively. It allows you to foster an environment where they feel empowered to innovate rather than held back by self-doubt or ingrained thought patterns. But individual awareness alone isn't enough.

We've seen how unlocking individual creativity is key to innovation. But no one innovates in isolation. The real challenge is how these creative individuals work together within teams, where ideas can either flourish or be stifled.

Now, we shift our focus to the **group level**. Individuals make up groups, and groups are where innovation either thrives or gets stuck. Teams can be formal, structured by the organization, or informal, emerging organically through workplace relationships. Both play a critical role in shaping an innovative culture.

Groups go through natural stages – forming, storming, norming, and performing [50] – but when it comes to innovation, two factors stand out: **diversity and psychological safety**.

A team's ability to innovate depends on the mix of perspectives in the room and whether those perspectives are voiced and heard. Diversity fuels creativity, but only if teams create an environment where differences lead to collaboration rather than conflict. That's why in the next two chapters, we'll explore how to build diverse teams and, just as importantly, how to create the psychological safety needed for them to thrive.

Let's start with diversity: why it matters, the challenges it brings, and how leaders can turn it into an advantage.

Chapter 4
Diversity

Walking down any supermarket aisle, have you ever seen a deodorant strictly designed for people with disabilities?

You're met with a wall of choices: chamomile, fresh scent, apple, cucumber, long-lasting formulas promising 48 or even 72 hours of protection, and even scents tailored for athletes – the list goes on. At first glance, it seems like there's plenty of diversity. But is there?

One of the most powerful drivers of innovation in teams is diversity. But diversity isn't just about representation, it's about seeing and solving problems differently. And often, we don't realize what's missing until we experience it ourselves.

The illusion of choice: are we really designing for everyone?

Despite the endless variety, I've never seen a deodorant designed specifically for people with disabilities. And, to be honest, I had never really thought about it. Like most people, I browse the shelves looking for what suits me best, without considering whether these everyday products are equally accessible to someone with limited mobility or different physical needs. And why would I? No one in my family faces these challenges, so their reality is largely invisible to me.

But that's exactly why diversity matters because our personal experiences shape what we notice and what we overlook. Without exposure to different perspectives, we assume that what works for us must work for everyone. Diversity challenges us to break free from functional fixedness, the mental shortcuts that limit our ability to see beyond our own experiences. By embracing different perspectives, we can design solutions that serve a broader range of people.

Figure 6: Inclusive design: deodorant for people with disabilities.
Source: Based on Unilever's commercial [51]. Illustrated by Sara Haugereid.

I was reminded of this when I came across Unilever's Rexona commercial for a deodorant designed specifically for consumers with disabilities. Seeing that image for the first time, I felt a wave of shame, I had never considered how something as simple as using deodorant could be a struggle for someone with limited dexterity. It was a humbling realization: what is 'normal' for one person can be an obstacle for another. This same principle applies far beyond consumer products. In organizations, leadership teams often design workplace policies, career paths, and innovation strategies based on what feels 'normal' to them without realizing who they might be leaving out.

This realization extends far beyond deodorant aisles. It plays out in workplaces every day. When teams are made up of people with similar backgrounds, experiences, and ways of thinking, they risk falling into the same trap – designing solutions for an 'average' user, that looks like them, while overlooking the needs of others. But diverse teams, by their very nature, bring in perspectives that challenge these blind spots, leading to better, more inclusive innovation.

This issue isn't just about consumer products, it extends to how we structure our businesses, teams, and even the way we approach problem-solving and moreover, how we innovate. Too often, companies design for an imagined 'average person' without realizing that this one-size-fits-all approach inevitably excludes large portions of the population.

The danger of designing for the 'average person'

Most products in supermarkets are designed for an 'average person.' This so-called 'average person' represents an oversimplified composite of traits deemed typical within a population. All deviations are erased, resulting in a one-size-fits-all version of the market. The larger the population, the greater the oversimplification, and the more needs and characteristics that get overlooked or excluded. Why is this problematic? Because designing products based on these generalizations can lead us to overlook important customer segments. We assume the wrong things about our customers and even suffer financial losses as a result.

Designing products for an 'average person' is like producing only one shoe size: the average size for the whole population. It might fit those who wear that specific size perfectly, but for everyone else, the shoe would be either too small or too big. Some might tolerate a slightly oversized shoe, but most would feel frustrated, wondering why only a select segment gets a perfect fit. The same applies to deodorant and countless other products, services, or technologies. **By designing an oversimplified 'average', businesses don't just exclude potential customers, they limit their own market reach and profitability.** Inclusive design isn't just ethical; it's a business imperative.

Here's what we'll explore together in this chapter:

▶ Why diversity is more than representation – it's a driver of better innovation, decision-making, and resilience.

▶ How different types of diversity shape team performance.

▶ The specific benefits and challenges of gender diversity, including underrepresentation, unconscious bias, and the double-bind dilemma.

▶ Practical ways leaders can break down barriers and build inclusive environments where diversity leads to real innovation.

▶ Why passive support isn't enough – how to make diversity a business driver, not just a compliance checkbox.

By the end, you'll have a clearer understanding of how to move beyond surface-level diversity and create conditions where different perspectives lead to stronger, smarter, and more innovative teams.

Why diversity matters: breaking free from blind spots

For example, the Association of American Medical Colleges published an article in 2021 revealing that most drugs have been tested primarily on white men [52]. However, women, particularly women of colour, differ significantly in their physiology, with unique hormonal patterns and physical characteristics. This means that these groups might have entirely different reactions to some drugs. This is why diversity matters. Only by embracing diversity can we begin to understand the needs and challenges of people different from the 'average person'. This inclusiveness opens doors to new products, services, ways of thinking and new income.

At the same time, companies are becoming increasingly global, serving diverse markets around the world. Likewise, the workforce is more mobile than ever, moving not just between cities but across countries, regions, and continents. With this movement, employees bring their unique cultures, languages, norms, and values into new workplaces, enriching their teams with varied perspectives. As a result, teams and workplaces are growing more diverse.

Diversity in teams: more perspectives, better solutions

A diverse team brings a wider array of perspectives. Imagine a group of people at a table – all of the same gender, age, hometown, university background, and even supporting the same football club. The chances of this group approaching a problem from different angles are low. Similarly, consider an environment with constant conditions: 36 degrees Celsius, all year round, no wind, no snow, no rain, just sun. What do you get? A desert. But introduce a mixture of sun, wind, rain, high and low temperatures, ice, and snow, and you create a flourishing garden with a rich, diverse plant life. Similarly, diversity within a team fosters a vibrant environment ripe for creativity and innovation.

What diverse teams can achieve?

When organizations successfully embrace diversity, they gain more than representation – they unlock a wide range of performance, collaboration, and innovation benefits. Research highlights the following advantages of diverse teams [53, 54, 55, 56, 57]:

> ▶ Diverse teams introduce varied viewpoints, which enhance creativity, improve decision-making, and strengthen strategic thinking. In contrast, homogeneous teams may experience less friction but often suffer from groupthink, limiting their problem-solving capacity.

▶ Cultural diversity in leadership improves alignment with global markets and enables more nuanced customer understanding.

▶ Different types of diversity add depth to discussions by bringing a wider range of perspectives, experiences, and interpretations to the table.

▶ Age-diverse teams balance experience with fresh thinking, helping to mitigate overconfidence and encourage more robust debate.

▶ Diverse teams generate more innovative solutions, particularly in knowledge-intensive fields like R&D and product development.

▶ Diversity supports adaptability, equipping teams to better respond to complexity and change.

From investing to teamwork: why variety strengthens resilience

Another way to understand the value of diversity is to compare it to a well-balanced investment portfolio. Just as portfolio diversity protects against volatility, team diversity protects against narrow thinking and functional fixedness. Through that diversity within a team builds resilience, fosters adaptability, and strengthens the foundation for creative and innovative solutions. It is not just a human issue; it is a strategic one.

Yet, achieving these outcomes isn't automatic. Without the right conditions, the advantages of diversity can remain untapped, or even turn into team challenges. Studies consistently show that homogeneous groups – made up of similar individuals – tend to display a more limited range of skills, ideas, and experiences than diverse, heterogeneous teams [58]. Combined with the Upper Echelons Theory which posits that the backgrounds and characteristics of top executives shape their decision-making, situation interpretation, and, in turn, the organization's behaviour and performance [58], this makes team composition, particularly its diversity, a crucial driver of a team's capacity for innovation.

But without inclusive management, diversity can lead to communication breakdowns, unresolved conflicts, and reduced cohesion.

Many studies show that having a diverse team doesn't automatically result in better performance, what matters is how diversity is leveraged. Inclusive leadership plays a critical role in ensuring that diverse voices are heard and valued. Organizations that actively address barriers, such as unconscious bias, stereotypes, and networking gaps, see the greatest benefits from diversity.

Understanding diversity isn't just about representation, it's about creating teams that thrive, innovate, and drive business success.

The psychology behind how we see differences

When we meet someone new, our instinct is to assess how they relate to us. We might notice differences in height, language, or non-verbal cues, such as whether they smile when speaking. When we see someone new, our brain quickly draws on past experiences and initial observations to place them into a category we believe matches who they are. We do this almost automatically, based only on initial observations, which then shapes how we interact, connect, or create distance.

When we find common traits with others, we tend to use these shared qualities as a foundation for building connections. This same phenomenon occurs within groups: each individual, consciously or unconsciously, evaluates others based on degrees of similarity and difference. Naturally, we gravitate toward those with whom we share common ground, forming friendships around these traits. This tendency can sometimes lead to the formation of subgroups within the larger team, a process known as social categorization [59].

However, it's important to recognize that social categorization can lead to internal conflicts, potentially hindering interaction and cooperation among team members [59]. While diversity can enhance a team's performance and creativity, it can also introduce friction that disrupts team dynamics.

So, should we strive for diversity even if it introduces challenges? Absolutely. The most innovative teams aren't those that avoid differences, but those that learn how to navigate and harness them effectively.

What is diversity?

While homogeneous teams may operate with less friction, they often lack the range of perspectives that drive creativity. Diverse teams, on the other hand, bring together a variety of experiences, skills, and viewpoints that lead to richer discussions, better decision-making, and ultimately, stronger innovation.

To understand how diversity influences teams, we need to break it down into different dimensions. Diversity isn't just about what we see, some differences are immediately visible, while others emerge over time through deeper interaction. Some forms of diversity impact team dynamics from the start, while others shape collaboration and innovation in more subtle ways.

In this section, I will explore how researchers categorize diversity and why these classifications matter for teamwork.

Homogenous and heterogeneous teams

Think about a team where everyone has the same background, education, and life experiences. It might feel easy to work together, but the risk is clear: limited perspectives, fewer ideas, and a tendency to reinforce existing beliefs rather than challenge them. Research consistently shows that while homogeneous teams may have less conflict, they also struggle with innovation [58]. In contrast, heterogeneous (diverse) groups bring together individuals with different backgrounds, perspectives, and experiences. Some differences, such as gender or nationality, are visible, while others, like work styles or cognitive approaches, become apparent only through deeper interaction.

Interestingly, a team can be both diverse and homogeneous, depending on which attributes we examine [60]. For example, a group of engineers from the same university may seem diverse in terms of personality, but homogenous in terms of professional background or gender. Understanding this complexity is essential for leaders aiming to build truly innovative teams.

Surface-level and deep-level diversity

Diversity, at its core, refers to the presence of differences within a group. Merriam-Webster dictionary defines it as 'the condition of having or being composed of different elements; a variety' [61]. In the context of teams, Van Knippenberg and Schippers expand on this, defining diversity as 'a characteristic of social grouping that reflects objective or subjective differences between group members' [59]. Put simply, diversity includes both what we see, like age or gender, and what we discover over time, such as cognitive styles and values.

For example, when meeting a new colleague, you immediately notice their gender, age, or nationality (surface-level traits) [53]. But over time, you discover their problem-solving approach, leadership style, or openness to risk (deep-level traits) [60]. While surface-level diversity influences first impressions, deep-level diversity ultimately determines how well a team collaborates and innovates [60].

Understanding both surface-level and deep-level diversity helps leaders foster teams that embrace differences not just at a demographic level, but in the way they think, problem-solve, and communicate. Understanding diversity isn't just about recognizing differences – it's about knowing how they interact [54]. Some dimensions of diversity enhance innovation more than others, and some require active inclusion strategies to unlock their full value [54]. In the next section, we'll explore the key diversity dimensions that shape teamwork and innovation.

Different dimensions of diversity

To fully understand how diversity impacts team performance, we can break it down into three key dimensions. Each dimension influences collaboration, innovation, and leadership differently, making it essential for organizations to recognize and manage them effectively. A practical way to categorize diversity in teams is by focusing on three key dimensions [6]:

1. Demographic diversity: readily observable attributes like ethnicity, age, and gender.

2. Psychological diversity: differences in problem-solving abilities, personality traits, and cognitive styles.

3. Informational diversity: variation in education, functional background, and industry experience.

While demographic diversity is the most visible, research shows that psychological and informational diversity are equally, if not more, critical for innovation.

Each of these dimensions impacts team performance in distinct ways [53, 54, 55, 56, 57]:

▶ Demographic diversity improves a team's ability to understand diverse customer segments and global markets, but may also require more effort to manage communication and cohesion.

▶ Psychological diversity fuels creativity and problem-solving by introducing varied ways of thinking and decision-making, though it may also lead to tension if not properly managed.

▶ Informational diversity enhances strategic execution and cross-functional collaboration by drawing on diverse experiences and areas of expertise, helping teams tackle complex challenges more effectively.

Each diversity dimension presents both opportunities and challenges. What they all have in common is their ability to expand perspectives, challenge conventional thinking, and drive organizational growth. **The real question isn't whether diversity is beneficial, it's how we create workplaces that fully harness its power.**

In the next section, we turn to gender diversity – one of the most widely discussed, yet still deeply imbalanced, aspects of workplace inclusion. Despite making up half the population and playing a crucial role in society, women remain significantly underrepresented in leadership and decision-making positions.

Gender diversity

Among the many dimensions of diversity, gender remains one of the most widely discussed and yet persistently imbalanced aspects of workplace inclusion.

Imagine someone offering you ten candidates for a leadership position but insisting you can only consider five of them. Wouldn't that seem like a wasted opportunity? Wouldn't you be afraid of missing the best candidate, and wanting to see the remaining five? Yet, this is exactly what happens in the job market, especially when it comes to women in top leadership positions.

Despite making up half the population, a significant portion of the workforce, acquiring and having same competencies as men, women are still severely underrepresented in leadership roles. This raises critical questions about fairness, talent utilization, and business impact.

An everlasting debate

Gender diversity is one of the most widely studied and debated aspects of workplace diversity. It is often used as a benchmark for broader diversity discussions because it highlights both the benefits, and the persistent challenges organizations face in achieving true inclusion.

On one side, research strongly supports the business case for gender-diverse teams, showing improved problem-solving, innovation, and financial performance. On the other side, discussions about tokenism, bias, and meritocracy complicate the conversation. The challenge is not just increasing representation, it's about ensuring that diversity leads to meaningful impact and sustainable change. Given its prominence, gender diversity serves as an insightful lens through which we can explore the broader implications of diversity management and its impact on team dynamics, innovation, and overall performance.

Gender diversity refers to the ratio of one gender in relation to the other within a team [62 cited in 53]. When one gender is significantly underrepresented, for example, men in nursing or women in fisheries and top management, these teams are considered gender-homogeneous [53]. Gender, however, is a more complex and multifaceted demographic factor compared to other variables such as age, education, functional background, or seniority within a management team. This complexity stems from the way gender shapes our social experiences, interactions, and environments, which, in turn, influence cognitive development, thinking, and behaviours [63 cited in 58].

It's also important to acknowledge that gender diversity is a two-way issue. While women are underrepresented in leadership and male-dominated fields, men remain significantly underrepresented in professions like nursing and education. However, this section will focus primarily on the barriers and effects of increasing female representation in leadership, as women, particularly women of colour, continue to be excluded from the highest levels of corporate decision-making. And when women are excluded from leadership, it can limit an organization's potential income, market insight, and overall competitiveness.

The gender leadership gap: where do women stand?

Despite earning 60% of master degrees [64], and making up nearly of 50% of the workplace, women hold only 10.4% of Fortune 500 CEO positions, with less than 1% being women of colour [65]. Even in medicine, where almost 60% of medical students are women [66], only one-third go on to become practicing doctors [67].

The pattern is clear: **women enter the workforce in strong numbers but disappear as roles become more senior**. They disappear from positions where they can impact innovation more strongly.

Interestingly, while white men hold up to one third of entry-level roles, their representation nearly doubles by the C-suite [68]. Why does women's representation decline as roles become more senior, despite achieving equal or higher education levels than men? Why do we keep choosing leaders from a smaller, male-dominated talent pool, especially when the broader, often equally or more qualified female pool is right there?

The argument for selecting men often centres on competencies. But logically, wouldn't a larger talent pool produce more qualified candidates due to greater competition?

This strong imbalance is a call to action, not only to ensure equal opportunities, but to recognize that a more diverse leadership pipeline could unlock untapped potential and drive meaningful progress in business leadership. The imbalance isn't just about fairness, it's a missed opportunity. And businesses that recognize this opportunity are already seeing results. Studies consistently show that companies with gender-diverse teams outperform their competitors in key areas ranging from innovation to financial success.

The business case: why gender-diverse teams perform better

Even when women enter leadership roles, gender diversity can introduce additional team challenges that organizations must manage effectively [69]. These challenges are conflict and communication issues, stereotyping women's role and behaviour, not enough significance and approval given to female participation [69]. However, research agrees that these **obstacles are far outweighed by the advantages that gender diversity brings to teams**. Moreover, these obstacles are not unbeatable. Organizations that actively recognize and address these barriers will be the ones that unlock the full potential of gender diversity.

Companies with more than 30% women executives consistently outperform those with fewer women in leadership roles [70]. The reason? A broader range of perspectives leads to better decision-making, smarter risk management, and greater adaptability in a rapidly changing business environment. Studies consistently show that companies with gender-diverse teams benefit from stronger financial performance, better decision-making, and increased innovation [54].

▶ Enhanced problem-solving and creativity: women bring unique knowledge, perspectives, and cognitive styles that enhance a team's ability to solve complex problems [58, 69]. Research suggests that gender-diverse teams are more likely to identify connections between seemingly unrelated ideas, leading to more innovative solutions and better resource allocation [71, 72, 73].

▶ Stronger leadership and team performance: female leaders are more likely to engage in transformational leadership, motivating and inspiring teams, while male leaders often adopt transactional leadership styles focused on structure and rewards. A blend of both leadership approaches fosters a stronger, more adaptive team culture [72, 74].

▶ Market insights and consumer understanding: women make up a significant share of global consumers, and companies with gender-diverse teams are better positioned to understand diverse market needs. Studies show that gender-balanced teams develop products and services that better align with consumer expectations, leading to stronger brand loyalty and sales performance [75].

▶ Inclusivity and organizational trust: workplaces that embrace gender diversity tend to have more open communication, stronger collaboration, and higher employee engagement. A welcoming and inclusive team environment encourages knowledge-sharing, enhances stakeholder relationships, and improves overall company reputation [58, 69].

Real-life example: Nanobit – how inclusion drives market growth

Here is a clear example of what inclusion means in business terms – specifically, in profit terms. Nanobit, a Croatian startup founded in 2008 by software engineers Alan Sumina and Zoran Vučinić, became a global success story when it was acquired by Swedish gaming giant Stillfront Group AB in 2020 [76]. While the acquisition amount was not publicly disclosed, Nanobit had already made its mark as an award-winning studio with millions of users worldwide.

What made the difference? Nanobit discovered that inclusion isn't just a social value – it's a strategic advantage. In its early years, the company focused primarily on building games for a traditionally male gamer audience. But after limited commercial success, they noticed an underserved market segment: female gamers [77]. Shifting their strategy, Nanobit began designing games specifically with women in mind.

The results? Their most successful titles are those targeted at female players [77]. And they are not alone in this. In 2020, women accounted for nearly 41% of all gamers in the U.S. and 48% in Asia [78]. Female gamers are not just a niche group – they are a massive, growing market.

Nanobit recognized what many still overlook: inclusion expands markets. By designing with diverse audiences in mind, they unlocked a new revenue stream that propelled them toward unicorn status.

Numerous studies have shown that female gamers often have different motivations and behaviours compared to their male counterparts. For example, research suggests that American women often play for achievement and social reasons – to engage socially and maintain relationships – while men are more likely to play for stress relief and competitive success [78]. In France, female gamers report playing to challenge themselves, while French males play more for stress management. Taiwanese studies show that women play for achievement and social engagement, while men play more to pass the time [78].

Game developers who understand these differences can design better, more inclusive experiences and grow their customer base in the process.

The numbers speak for themselves. The global video gaming industry was valued at USD 249.55 billion in 2022 and is projected to reach USD 665.77 billion by 2030, growing at a CAGR of 13.1%. Asia-Pacific led the market in 2022, accounting for over 46% of the global share [79].

Inclusion isn't just about fairness, it's about foresight. It's about recognizing emerging markets, responding to real user needs, and designing products that reflect the diversity of the world we live in. Nanobit's success is a vivid reminder that when companies embrace inclusion, they don't just do good, they do well.

Gender diversity isn't just an ethical priority, it's a strong competitive edge that drives real results. Studies confirm that firms with gender-diverse leadership outperform their industry peers in profitability, innovation efficiency, and stakeholder trust [69, 80 cited in 54]. But despite the evidence, barriers remain. In the next section, I will explore the challenges holding women back.

Barriers to gender diversity

Despite progress in gender diversity, **deep-rooted barriers continue to hold women back, many of which operate subtly, shaping decisions and opportunities without people even realizing it.** While these challenges affect multiple dimensions of diversity, two of the most persistent obstacles for women in leadership stand out: unconscious bias and the double-bind dilemma.

Unconscious bias

Unconscious bias shapes how we evaluate leadership potential. Studies show that men are often promoted based on their potential, while women are expected to prove their competence before being considered for leadership roles.

I've heard countless stories from men proudly sharing how they landed senior leadership roles or board memberships in their 30s with no prior experience. They would confidently share: 'I was young, I had no idea what I was doing, but I got the opportunity, and I embraced it.' Yet, when a woman applies for the same role, the conversation shifts dramatically. Suddenly, it's about competence, people argue: 'We should focus on skills, not gender.'

But why weren't these same competence concerns raised when men were given leadership opportunities before they were 'ready'? The reality is that men are often forgiven for lacking experience, seen as promising, ambitious risk-takers, while women are expected to meet higher standards before even being considered.

This isn't just anecdotal; it's backed by research. McKinsey's 'Women in the Workplace' report [81] confirms that men are promoted based on potential, while women must first prove their competence. This fundamental bias slows women's career progression and reinforces leadership imbalances.

Beyond unconscious bias, women in leadership face another challenge: the expectation paradox. Even when women break through to leadership roles, they face contradictory standards that make success an uphill battle.

The double-bind dilemma: A no-win situation for women in leadership

Women in leadership often face a no-win situation, commonly referred to as the double-bind dilemma. Research shows that [82]:

▶ If women are assertive, they are labelled 'aggressive' or 'too dominant.'

▶ If women are collaborative, they are seen as 'too soft' or 'lacking authority.'

▶ Men exhibiting the same behaviours are praised as 'strong leaders' and seen as confident and decisive.

This contradiction forces women to carefully balance their leadership style, often limiting their ability to lead authentically [82].

This double standard means women are held to higher performance standards while receiving less credit for their leadership contributions, creating an invisible barrier that slows their progress into senior roles [83].

Leadership advancement isn't just about skill, it's about access to the right networks. Men have traditionally benefited from informal sponsorship and mentorship circles, where senior leaders advocate for their promotions. Women, however, are less likely to receive sponsorship from top executives, leaving them without key advocates for leadership opportunities [84]. Research identifies several reasons why women are less likely to receive sponsorship from top executives, including:

▶ Sponsors fearing reputational risk if the woman is not seen as a conventional leadership fit [84].

▶ Sponsorship is often forged in informal settings where women aren't always present or invited [85].

▶ Affinity bias, the tendency to support those who are similar, causes male leaders to sponsor other men more often [68].

▶ The lack of formal sponsorship programs amplifies the problem, as women are more reliant on informal networks that often exclude them [68].

Without these career sponsors, climbing the leadership ladder becomes significantly harder.

Real-world reflections on diversity

Diversity is essential for long-term sustainability and innovation, yet many organizations still struggle to make it a core part of their business practices. While some companies have successfully embedded diversity into their strategies, others lag far behind. For example, Unilever's focus on inclusive product design, such as deodorants for people with disabilities, showcases how diversity can be integrated into a company's strategy. Similarly, Norwegian energy company Equinor actively promotes diversity in its hiring practices.

However, misunderstandings and outdated practices persist. In 2022, a Norwegian public institution included requests for nationality and age in its public tender applications, claiming this would help assess a consultant's proficiency in Norwegian [86]. This approach fails to recognize that factors like citizenship or age often have little to do with language skills. Equinor, on the other hand, seeks similar data to enhance diversity consciously and effectively [86].

Other companies face different challenges. The Norwegian branch of McKinsey, for example, has struggled to appoint female partners, with its CEO stating at the Arendal Conference in 2022 that 'they cannot find women interested in the role.' Rather, a more constructive approach might be to explore what internal organizational and external factors could be discouraging women from pursuing partnership opportunities. In contrast, PwC Norway has now regularly appointed women as partners, demonstrating that gender diversity at the leadership level is achievable with the right culture and policies.

In Norway, a 2023 law now mandates that companies meeting certain thresholds must ensure at least 40% of board positions are held by individuals of different genders. A move expected to open around 13,000 board seats for women. However, resistance remains, with one Norwegian leader stating at a conference in 2024 that '13,000 of us men are not going anywhere' [86].

Unfortunately, some leaders are only recently recognizing the value of diversity. A CEO of a major Norwegian investment institution acknowledged on LinkedIn in November 2023 [86] that a newly published report finally proves that gender diversity drives profitability, a conclusion supported by decades of earlier research. Yet, when I reached out to discuss this with him, rather than engaging directly with me, he tagged a male colleague. This subtle, probably unintentional, but telling example of how traditional leadership dynamics persist, even among those who claim to support diversity.

This response underscores a deeper issue: even leaders who recognize the importance of diversity may unintentionally perpetuate traditional dynamics, where male voices are prioritized. This highlights the need not only for structural diversity, but also for an active commitment to inclusive practices in everyday interactions, especially at the leadership level.

As some nations push forward on diversity, others are pulling back. The U.S., once a leader in corporate DEI (diversity, equality, inclusion) initiatives, is now witnessing a sharp reversal, raising concerns about the long-term commitment to diversity in business and education. Their recent political shifts have led to a rollback of DEI efforts, particularly in corporate and academic spaces. Even the Norwegian Research Council has expressed concern, calling the situation in the U.S. 'dramatic' and warning that the rollback of DEI efforts could have serious consequences for international research collaboration and scientific progress [87].

After years of progress, several states have passed legislation limiting DEI programs in universities and businesses, arguing that these initiatives promote exclusion rather than inclusion. This shift threatens to reverse progress in workplace equity, limit diverse talent pipelines, and weaken innovation by narrowing perspectives at decision-making levels.

For women, these examples are more than just setbacks – they are signals. We push forward, we work harder, we break barriers, only to be overlooked, unheard, and dismissed. Over time, the message becomes clear: fighting for a seat at the table often leads to the same result – being ignored. And so, many of us step back, not because we lack ambition, but because we see that the effort leads nowhere.

But when women pull back, the cycle continues. Leadership teams remain homogenous, their perspectives on customers and innovation unchallenged. **The absence of diversity reinforces functional fixedness, where the same ideas circulate among the same people, limiting creativity and strategic growth.** In the end, organizations don't just lose female talent, they lose the ability to see beyond their own narrow viewpoints and hence missing new business opportunities.

Biases toward female-led initiatives persist in other contexts as well. A recent article in *The New York Times* pointed out that venture capital firms focusing exclusively on women-led startups are often questioned for allegedly prioritizing gender over competence [88]. Yet, the same argument rarely arises for male-led firms that invest predominantly in male-owned ventures. Again, double standard highlights the ongoing bias that women-led companies and initiatives still face.

In short, while progress is being made, it will take time to convince male leaders that diversity is not only effective, but should become the norm at all organizational levels. Encouragingly, more companies are recognizing these benefits, and more advocates are championing diversity openly and proactively. But leaders cannot be passive observers. They must actively shape inclusive cultures, challenge outdated norms, and embed diversity into everyday business strategy. The future of innovation depends on it.

Conclusion: driving innovation through inclusive leadership

Diversity is not just a moral imperative, it's a strategic advantage that fuels innovation, adaptability, and business growth. Yet, despite the overwhelming evidence supporting the benefits of diverse teams, barriers persist. Unconscious bias, outdated leadership structures, and exclusionary workplace cultures continue to hold back progress.

For organizations to truly harness the power of diversity, they must move beyond surface-level representation and focus on inclusion, equity, and structural change. Diversity without inclusion is merely optics, it is only when different perspectives are heard, valued, and integrated into decision-making that real innovation emerges.

The challenge is clear, but so is the opportunity. Leaders who actively break down barriers, champion inclusion, and create environments where diversity thrives will not only build stronger, but more creative teams also – they will drive the next generation of breakthrough innovations.

Key takeaways from this chapter

▶ Diversity is not just about representation, it's a strategic driver of innovation, adaptability, and business performance.

▶ Different types of diversity – demographic, psychological, and informational – each contribute uniquely to team creativity and problem-solving.

▶ Gender diversity remains one of the most persistent challenges, with unconscious bias, double standards, and lack of sponsorship still limiting women's advancement.

▶ Diverse teams outperform when leaders actively create inclusive environments where all voices are heard, valued, and integrated into decision-making.

▶ To move from optics to impact, leaders must embed diversity into strategy, challenge fixed assumptions, and lead with intentional inclusion.

So, what can you do as a leader?

Five key steps a leaders can take to foster diversity and innovation

1. Move beyond hiring diversity – ensure inclusion in decision-making

Simply having diverse individuals on a team isn't enough. They must be empowered to influence decisions. More on that in the next chapter.

How to implement:

▶ Actively invite diverse voices into key strategy meetings, not just HR discussions.

▶ Engage actively in rotating who leads team discussions and presentations to give everyone a platform.

▶ Regularly review who is speaking and being heard: is the same group always leading conversations?

2. Challenge the 'potential vs. competence' bias in leadership promotions
As seen in the chapter, men are often promoted based on potential, while women must prove competence.

How to implement:

▶ Review promotion decisions: are women and minorities being held to higher standards?

▶ Train managers to recognize unconscious bias in leadership assessments.

▶ Create sponsorship programs, not just mentorship. Leaders should advocate for diverse talent at senior levels.

3. Break the cycle of functional fixedness in teams
Leadership teams that exclude diverse voices become stuck in the same perspectives, limiting creativity.

How to implement:

▶ Form cross-functional, cross-background teams to drive innovation.

▶ Bring in external advisors from underrepresented backgrounds for fresh insights.

▶ Encourage leaders to seek dissenting opinions rather than reinforcing their own views.

4. Make diversity a business driver, not just an HR metric
Many organizations still see diversity as a compliance issue rather than a competitive advantage.

How to implement:

- ▷ Use diverse teams to test new products, services, and marketing approaches.

- ▷ Reward leaders and teams who successfully integrate diversity into innovation efforts.

- ▷ Tie diversity goals to business KPIs, e.g., innovation output, bonuses, salary, market expansion, customer insights.

5. Address the DEI backlash proactively – don't be a passive observer
With the rollback of DEI efforts in some regions, leaders must reinforce their commitment to inclusion.

How to implement:

- ▷ Be transparent about the company's stance on DEI. Communicate why it matters.

- ▷ Develop diversity strategies that are deeply embedded in business goals, so they are harder to dismantle.

- ▷ Equip managers with data-driven arguments on how diversity improves profitability and innovation.

Diversity is not just an HR policy, it's a business strategy that fuels creativity, competitiveness, and long-term success. It is a leader's mandate to walk the talk, to actively dismantle barriers, empower diverse voices, and embed inclusion into business practices. Because diversity doesn't just build stronger teams, it shapes the future of innovation.

In the next chapter, we'll delve into the critical importance of team climate and psychological safety. These elements foster communication openness and trust, creating a foundation where diverse teams can leverage their differences for optimal innovation outcomes.

***

For additional tools related to this chapter, visit: vinco.no/ future-fit-innovation-resources

Chapter 5
Psychological safety

During an annual condominium meeting, at the end, the leader asked if anyone had any suggestions or questions. I spoke up: 'How about we convert a portion of our common storage into a small gym?'. My idea was met with uncomfortable silence, and eventually, the leader responded hesitantly: 'I honestly don't know how to address that', before promptly closing the meeting. In that moment, I began doubting myself, wondering, 'Was my idea really that bad? Was it stupid?'.

Years later, small gyms in condominiums became a popular trend adding real value to properties. Yet, in that meeting, my suggestion had been dismissed, not because it was bad, but because the environment wasn't open to new suggestions.

This happens in organizations, too. History is filled with companies that shut down or ignored ideas – Kodak dismissing digital photography, Nokia resisting smartphone innovation, Volkswagen's internal culture silencing concerns on CO_2 emissions – leading to missed opportunities and major failures.

The cost of dismissive cultures is high. If people don't feel safe to speak up, businesses don't just lose engagement, they lose innovation, competitive advantage, and even credibility.

You've gathered a diverse group of people around the table. That's it, right? Now your team will be super innovative. Not exactly. Because how can you be sure they will speak up?

Diversity alone doesn't guarantee innovation. Just because you have different perspectives in the room doesn't mean people will automatically collaborate, challenge ideas, or produce great results. In fact, they might do the opposite: stay silent, withdraw, or even clash.

In the previous chapter, I mentioned that **diversity can create friction**, particularly around communication and conflict. Every article I read for that chapter agreed: **these issues aren't caused by diversity itself but by poor diversity management** and, more importantly, by a lack of psychological safety.

Diversity without inclusion leads to fragmentation. The key is to create environments where diverse perspectives contribute meaningfully to decision-making and innovation.

That's why this chapter is about exactly that: creating a team environment where people feel safe to speak up, take risks, and contribute fully to your organizational innovation efforts. However, research also shows that these conditions aren't viable in the longer-term without innovation strategy [54].

Psychological safety: the missing ingredient

Think about the teams you've been part of throughout your life. Some were lively and filled with energy, where people felt comfortable sharing ideas and challenging each other. Others were quiet and cautious, where only the safest topics like weather were discussed, and mistakes were hidden rather than learned from.

Maybe you've heard statements like:

▶ 'We don't bring problems to the table.'

▶ 'I only want good news in meetings.'

These attitudes shut down innovation and create a chilling effect. When people fear criticism, dismissal, or ridicule, they hold back, and that's when teams fail to reach their potential.

But in a psychologically safe team the opposite happens. People feel encouraged to speak up, share bold ideas, and challenge the status quo. And that's exactly what drives innovation.

In this chapter, you'll discover:

▶ What psychological safety really means (and what it's not).

▶ The science behind it and why it's crucial for innovation.

▶ How leaders can build a psychologically safe culture.

▶ Practical steps to increase psychological safety in your team.

By the end of the chapter, you'll have a clear roadmap to unlock the full potential of your diverse team and drive real innovation.

Let's get started.

What is psychological safety?

You've probably been in meetings where some people openly share ideas, while others stay silent. Maybe you've had an idea but hesitated to speak up, wondering: *Will this sound stupid? Will they dismiss me? What if they think I don't know what I'm talking about?*

That hesitation, that moment of self-censorship, is exactly what psychological safety is about.

Defining psychological safety

The term psychological safety was popularized by Amy Edmondson, who defines it as: 'A shared belief that the team is safe for interpersonal risks.'

In other words, it's the confidence that you can speak up, ask questions, admit mistakes, or suggest new ideas without fear of embarrassment, rejection, or punishment.

The idea isn't new, though. Earlier research explored similar concepts:

▶ Carl Rogers in 1954 described psychological safety as an environment that cultivates self-worth, creating spaces where individuals feel valued and are free from external judgement [89].

▶ In 1965, Schein and Bennis described psychological safety as an individual's sense of security in the face of change [90].

▶ Wiliam Kahn (1990) [91] defined psychological safety as a state where individuals experience trusting and supportive interpersonal relationships with colleagues. This environment allows them to freely express themselves without fearing negative impacts on their self-image, status, or career [91].

The key difference? Kahn focused on the individual experience: safety in immediate relationships [91]. While Edmondson's (1999) shifted focus to teams, making psychological safety as 'a shared belief' or collective experience [92].

How does this translate to a team situation? This distinction is critical. You may personally feel confident, but if the team culture discourages speaking up, even the best ideas will remain unspoken.

The hidden cost of fear: why psychological safety matters

Psychological safety is not just about feeling comfortable, it's about creating a culture where ideas, concerns, and mistakes are openly discussed.

When it's missing, interpersonal risks, risks how we are perceived by others when we are expressing our ideas or perspectives [93], easily become career and growth risks:

▶ People stay silent, even when they see problems.

▶ They avoid asking for help, fearing it will make them look incompetent.

▶ They play it safe, avoiding bold ideas or controversial insights.

Like I did at that condominium meeting where the awkward silence made me instantly doubt myself, thinking, maybe it really was a stupid idea after all. So, at the next meeting, I stayed quiet. That's what fear does: it shuts us down. Just as it did in companies like Kodak or Nokia, where people saw disruption coming, but were afraid or simply not safe enough to push their ideas forward more persistently. And the consequences? Missed opportunities, stalled innovation, and often, irreversible decline.

What psychological safety is not?

It's important to clear up common misconceptions. Psychological safety:

▶ It's not about being 'nice' [94, 95 cited in 96]. Teams can (and should) have healthy conflict and debate. The goal is to create an environment where people feel safe challenging ideas, not just agreeing with everything.

▶ It's not the same as low accountability [97]. Some leaders think psychological safety means avoiding difficult conversations or criticism. In reality, the best teams have high psychological safety and high accountability; people support each other while also holding high standards.

▶ It's not about avoiding mistakes [97]. It's about learning from them. Companies with strong psychological safety acknowledge errors openly, using them as fuel for improvement [98].

We see this in action at Sparebanken Norge, where, as Siren Sundland shared, psychological safety is balanced with clear expectations, accountability, and strong openness to learning from mistakes.

Why is psychological safety critical for innovation?

Case study: Google's Project Aristotle

One of the strongest business cases for psychological safety comes from Google's Project Aristotle. Google wanted to crack the code on what makes teams successful. They analyzed over 180 teams, looking at everything from individual talent to leadership styles [99]. The result? Psychological safety was the number one factor distinguishing high-performing teams from the rest [99].

This finding reinforces a crucial truth: innovation thrives in teams where people feel psychologically safe. Without it, ideas go unspoken, constructive conflict turns destructive, and risk-taking is replaced by conformity.

Without psychological safety:

▶ Ideas go unspoken for fear of judgement.

▶ Constructive conflict turns into destructive conflict.

▶ Innovation is stifled because people stick to the safest route.

But with psychological safety:

▶ Teams engage in open debate without fear of backlash.

▶ People collaborate, take risks, and experiment.

▶ Innovation thrives because everyone feels empowered to contribute.

Innovation doesn't happen in isolation

Innovation requires risk-taking, open discussion, and collaboration, all of which depend on a culture where people feel safe to contribute freely.

At its core, innovation is a social process. It's about bringing together diverse ideas, challenging assumptions, and taking calculated risks to find better solutions [100, 101, 102 cited in 103]. But this process can only thrive if people feel safe enough to [104]:

▶ Propose unconventional or risky ideas, even if they seem far-fetched.

▶ Challenge the status quo without fear of backlash.

▶ Learn from failures without blame or embarrassment.

Psychological safety thus creates a foundation where team members are encouraged to fully engage in these behaviours, all of which are essential for sustaining innovation. Without psychological safety, negative responses like dismissal, resistance, or skepticism can lead innovation teams or individuals to become more cautious, reducing creative output, lowering their willingness to voice new ideas, and ultimately risking the success of innovation projects [105].

Research shows that when psychological safety is high, teams generate more breakthrough ideas, experiment more effectively, and improve continuously.

Innovation processes

Psychological safety plays a crucial role at every stage of innovation:

▶ Idea generation: employees feel free to propose bold, unconventional solutions without hesitation.

▶ Discussion and debate: teams engage in constructive disagreement rather than avoiding difficult conversations.

▶ Evaluation and prototyping: failure is seen as a learning opportunity, not a personal risk.

▶ Implementation: teams provide continuous feedback and iterate solutions without fear of blame.

Without psychological safety, employees may hold back ideas, avoid difficult conversations, or resist experimentation ultimately weakening the innovation process.

For business model innovation and entrepreneurship: PS is even more crucial

For organizations undergoing business model innovation (BMI) or entrepreneurship psychological safety is even more critical [104].

Entrepreneurship is an innovation at its most extreme: launching entirely new ventures in uncertain environments.

Unlike product or process innovations, BMI often involves questioning the company's entire foundation. It means [104]:

- ▶ Challenging long-standing assumptions.
- ▶ Experimenting with unproven business models.
- ▶ Facing high resistance to change, both internally and externally.

Studies by Chesbrough (2010) and Teece (2010) [106, 107 cited in 104] show that successful BMI requires extensive experimentation, failure, and learning, all of which demand psychological safety.

Similarly, Miao et al. (2019) found that employees who perceive psychological safety in their workplace are far more likely to engage in entrepreneurial activities [108].

Organizations that embed psychological safety into their innovation processes, whether in established businesses or startups, are better positioned to stay ahead of disruption.

High-performance work systems: embedding innovation into culture

Some organizations like Pixar, Toyota, Procter & Gamble, or Sparebanken Norge take psychological safety even further by embedding it into their organizational design implementing high-performance work systems.

High-performance work systems (HPWS) are designed to maximize innovation and engagement by fostering [109, 110, 111]:

▶ Psychological capital by nurturing confidence, resilience, and optimism.

▶ Psychological safety by creating an environment where people feel free to experiment.

▶ Supportive leadership through leaders who actively remove barriers to innovation.

Research by Kark and Carmeli (2009) shows that employees in HPWS are far more likely to engage in creativity and innovation [112], because they know they won't be punished for taking smart risks.

Psychological safety isn't just a 'nice-to-have', it's the foundation of every successful innovation culture. Organizations that prioritize it enable their teams to take smart risks, experiment fearlessly, and challenge conventional thinking. Whether through breakthrough products, new business models, or entrepreneurial ventures, companies with a psychologically safe culture will always be more adaptive, resilient, and innovative than those that operate in fear.

The role of leadership in creating psychological safety

Why leadership is the cornerstone of psychological safety?

Leaders set the tone for whether employees feel safe to speak up, take risks, and challenge ideas. Research consistently shows that leadership style is the most influential predictor of psychological safety environment [113 cited in 109].

Again, psychological safety isn't about 'being nice', it's about fostering open dialogue, accountability, and learning from mistakes. Leaders influence this climate through their daily interactions [114 cited in 115], shaping whether employees feel encouraged or discouraged to share ideas [116 cited in 117].

▶ Supportive leadership creates trust, allowing employees to express concerns, contribute ideas, and engage in constructive dialogue [118].

▶ Negative leadership behaviours, such as dismissing input or punishing mistakes, erode psychological safety, making employees more cautious and less innovative [119].

▶ Transformational leaders, who build strong relationships and remain accessible, are particularly effective in fostering an environment of trust and engagement [117].

By establishing clear norms, modelling vulnerability, and promoting openness, leaders unlock their team's full potential, making innovation, collaboration, and learning possible.

Five key leadership behaviours that foster psychological safety

Leaders play a crucial role in establishing norms that make team members feel safe to contribute. Research highlights five key leadership behaviours that directly impact psychological safety that I will present below.

1. Model vulnerability: leaders should admit mistakes and seek feedback

Leaders who acknowledge their limitations, admit mistakes, and actively seek feedback create an environment where employees feel safe doing the same. Feedback-seeking and feedback-sharing are critical behaviours that demonstrate openness and reduce hierarchical barriers [120, 118].

However, feedback-seeking alone is not enough. If leaders fail to act on the feedback they receive, employees lose trust, and psychological safety declines [118]. Instead, leaders should [118]:

▶ Share their responses to feedback transparently.

▶ Admit past mistakes and what they learned from them.

▶ Encourage employees to do the same, making team vulnerability a team norm.

By normalizing feedback-sharing, leaders reinforce trust and accountability, strengthening psychological safety [118].

2. Encourage open dialogue: active listening and leader humility
Leaders who listen actively encourage diverse opinions and value all contributions, foster a climate where employees feel heard and respected. Humble leadership is a key driver of this culture [121 cited in 122].

Humble leaders:

▶ Recognize the contributions of their team members.

▶ Remain open to alternative viewpoints and new ideas.

▶ Frame mistakes as learning opportunities rather than failures.

Teams led by humble leaders are more likely to challenge ideas, share concerns, and collaborate openly [121].

3. Set clear expectations and empower: psychological safety and autonomy
Leaders must create an environment where employees feel both safe and empowered. Empowering leadership, which includes granting autonomy, reducing bureaucratic barriers, and fostering ownership, enhances motivation and creativity [123 cited in 96; 124 cited in 105].

Psychological safety and empowerment work hand in hand:

▶ Without psychological safety, empowerment can feel like a burden rather than an opportunity.

▶ Without empowerment, psychological safety may not translate into action [125].

4. Demonstrate integrity: building trust through aligned actions
Psychological safety depends on trust – and trust is built when leaders consistently align their actions with their words. Behavioural integrity is a critical leadership trait that reinforces psychological safety [126]. Leaders who demonstrate integrity foster a culture where employees feel secure in speaking up.

When leaders act inconsistently, employees hesitate to take interpersonal risks [127 cited in 126].

Research shows that teams led by high-integrity leaders experience stronger collaboration, better problem-solving, and higher innovation levels [128].

5. Use humour wisely: strengthening vs. undermining psychological safety
The way leaders use humour can either enhance or erode psychological safety. Affiliative humour – positive, inclusive humour – helps build trust and fosters knowledge-sharing [129].

However, aggressive humour – mocking, sarcastic, chauvinistic, or belittling remarks – reduces psychological safety and discourages employees from speaking up [130 cited in 129].

Leaders should use humour to build connections, not create fear. Encouraging lightheartedness while maintaining respect strengthens team cohesion.

Key take aways

Leaders set the cultural tone for psychological safety.

▹ Humble leadership and vulnerability foster trust and openness.

▹ Empowerment and integrity drive team confidence and innovation.

▹ Humour should unify teams, not create discomfort.

By embedding these leadership behaviours into daily practice, you as a leader can create an environment where people feel safe to contribute, take risks, and innovate.

Leadership traps that destroy psychological safety

Even if you are a well-intentioned leader, you can unintentionally undermine psychological safety. Here are five common leadership traps to avoid:

1. Micromanaging: over-controlling employees creates fear of mistakes and discourages risk-taking. Instead of trusting teams to make decisions, micromanagers create a climate where employees play it safe.

2. Dismissing new ideas too quickly: when leaders shut down suggestions without consideration, employees learn to stay silent. Over time, this kills innovation and reduces engagement.

3. Creating a culture of fear: if employees believe speaking up carries negative consequences, they will withhold information, avoid accountability, and disengage. High-fear cultures lead to stagnation, poor decision-making, and missed opportunities.

4. Overconfidence without awareness: leaders who believe they are humble but fail to show it create misalignment between their self-perception and how employees actually experience them. Rego et al. (2021) found that this misalignment weakens psychological safety and damages trust [126].

5. Not acting on feedback: seeking feedback but failing to act on it is worse than not asking at all [118]. Employees see inconsistent follow-through as insincere, leading to distrust and disengagement [118].

Avoiding these traps will allow you as a leader to foster a culture of trust, learning, and open dialogue, ensuring psychological safety remains a foundation for innovation and growth.

Leadership, culture, and context: power distance considerations

Psychological safety is not one-size-fits-all – its effectiveness depends also on cultural context, particularly power distance, or the extent to which hierarchy is emphasized within a team or organization.

▷ Low power distance cultures: in cultures where hierarchy is less rigid, open discussion and flat structures are the norm. Leaders who encourage collaborative decision-making and open feedback are more likely to foster psychological safety [122].

▷ High power distance cultures: however, in hierarchical cultures, employees expect strong leadership and clear authority. If leaders rely too much on openness without reinforcing structure, it can create uncertainty or discomfort among employees [122].

To effectively foster your psychological safety in different power distance settings, you should:

▷ Recognize team expectations, balance openness with structure where needed.

▷ Encourage input in a culturally appropriate way, some teams may prefer indirect methods (e.g., anonymous feedback).

▷ Maintain clarity in roles and decision-making. This reduces uncertainty while promoting trust.

By adapting their leadership approach while upholding core psychological safety principles, leaders can create an inclusive and high-performing environment across diverse cultural contexts.

The dangers of low psychological safety: navigating voice and silence in the workplace

You're in a meeting. You have a valuable idea, but something holds you back. You glance around the room – no one else is speaking up. You decide to stay silent, fearing your suggestion might be dismissed or, worse, criticized. The meeting ends, and the problem remains unsolved. This is the reality of low psychological safety.

A similar scenario happened when I was leading a workshop for board members and the leadership team of a medium-size company. When I was talking about psychological safety, the CEO proudly said: 'We have strong psychological safety here.' When the workshop was finished and it was time for Q&A, I asked one silent member of the meeting: 'What do you think?' He answered: 'It does not matter what I think, they will not listen to me anyway.' To me it was clear that the psychological safety of the company is weak despite what the CEO believes.

In environments where psychological safety is weak, employees self-censor, withhold concerns, and disengage, leading to missed opportunities, reduced collaboration, and stagnation [118]. Without open communication, teams struggle to identify problems early, adapt to change, and drive innovation. Understanding how voice and silence function in the workplace is crucial to recognizing the hidden costs of fear-based cultures.

The cost of silence: how low psychological safety undermines teams

When employees fear judgement, criticism, or retaliation, they hesitate to share ideas or challenge decisions. Research highlights key consequences of low psychological safety:

▶ Loss of innovation: fear-driven cultures prevent employees from proposing new solutions, leading to stagnation and missed growth opportunities [131].

▶ Poor decision-making: when employees withhold critical concerns, teams fail to course-correct before problems escalate [132 cited in 131]. The Volkswagen CO_2 scandal? It became a major crisis for the company, as of 1 June 2020, the scandal had cost them $33.3 billion in fines, penalties, financial settlements, and buyback costs [133].

▶ Toxic work environments: without open dialogue, mistrust and misalignment grow, leading to strained relationships, low morale, and eventual turnover [134]. This can seriously damage your employer brand, leading prospective talent to avoid applying altogether.

▶ Process losses and reduced performance: teams lacking psychological safety fail to integrate diverse perspectives, leading to weaker collaboration and lower efficiency [92 cited in 131]. This can be seen in companies where a junior or minority team members hesitate to challenge flawed strategies leading to product flops and misaligned launches.

Over time, a culture of silence erodes engagement [131], driving high-performing employees to seek healthier, more inclusive workplaces [134].

Voice vs. silence: understanding workplace behaviour

Sherf et al. (2021) identify two key workplace behaviours [135]:

1. Voice: the intentional act of sharing ideas, concerns, or suggestions to improve the organization.

2. Silence: the deliberate withholding of information, often due to fear of negative consequences.

Psychological safety determines whether employees engage in voice or remain silent. Employees assess whether speaking up will lead to positive recognition or potential backlash, a process influenced by two psychological systems [135]:

1. A system that encourages voice when employees expect constructive change or reward – The Behaviour Activation System (BAS).

2. A system that triggers silence when employees perceive risk, punishment, or futility in speaking up – The Behaviour Inhibition System (BIS).

In low psychological safety environments, behaviours inhibition dominates, leading employees to self-protect rather than contribute.

The selective nature of voice

Interestingly, even in psychologically safe teams, not all employees speak up equally. Sherf et al. (2021) thus highlight that individuals [135]:

▶ Filter their concerns: only voicing issues they believe will lead to change.

▶ Assess risk constantly: choosing when, how, and if they should raise concerns.

▶ May appear silent when new: employees in their early weeks often withhold ideas until they understand team norms.

This means leaders cannot rely solely on what is spoken – they must actively identify unspoken issues and create safe activation experiences to encourage open dialogue [135].

Breaking the silence: creating a voice-enabling culture

Simply advocating for psychological safety isn't enough, leaders must also proactively address barriers to voice. Sherf et al. (2021) suggest [135]:

▶ Encouraging small, low-risk contributions: normalize speaking up with quick check-ins or anonymous feedback tools.

- ▶ Reinforcing follow-through: employees will continue voicing concerns only if they see their input leads to action.

- ▶ Shaping activation experiences: provide visible rewards for contribution to reinforce that speaking up is valued.

The true cost of fear-based cultures

Low psychological safety doesn't just harm individual employees, it cripples entire organizations. Fear-based cultures kill innovation, weaken decision-making, and drive talent away. The difference between a thriving team and a stagnant one often comes down to a simple question: *Are people afraid to speak up?* If the answer is yes, then silence isn't just a symptom, it's a warning sign.

However, while the core principles remain the same, how leaders and teams foster psychological safety must be adapted to fit their specific context as well.

Psychological safety in different work environments

Imagine working in a remote team where cameras stay off, messages are short, and responses take hours. You hesitate to share an idea because you're unsure how it will be received. Now picture an R&D team under pressure where mistakes are costly, deadlines are tight, and no one wants to risk speaking up. Psychological safety isn't just a leadership buzzword; its challenges and solutions vary across different work environments.

The challenge of psychological safety in remote and hybrid teams

The shift to remote and hybrid work has created new obstacles to psychological safety, as physical distance makes it harder to build trust. Sjöblom et al. (2022) emphasize that remote work can weaken informal communication and team cohesion, leading to less openness and increased hesitation to speak up [136].

In remote settings, team members may [136]:

▶ Fear of misinterpretation due to lack of non-verbal cues.

▶ Struggle with reduced feedback loops, making it harder to gauge responses.

▶ Experience social isolation, lowering trust and engagement.

How to Build Psychological Safety Remotely? Three simple steps include [136]:

1. Regular check-ins and virtual one-on-ones to maintain open communication.

2. Encouraging informal connections by creating digital spaces for casual discussions strengthens relationships.

3. Clear expectations and response norms: teams that set guidelines on how and when to communicate foster a sense of predictability and trust.

Without these intentional efforts, remote teams risk low engagement, decreased collaboration, and weakened innovation.

High-risk industries: the need for psychological safety in R&D

Innovation thrives when employees feel safe to challenge ideas and take risks. However, R&D teams and high-risk industries face additional hurdles: projects are very uncertain, time-sensitive, and high-stakes make mistakes costly.

Chandrasekaran and Mishra (2012) highlight that in R&D projects, high autonomy combined with high uncertainty can lead to psychological isolation, where employees hesitate to share concerns or collaborate effectively [134].

Key challenges in R&D teams are [134]:

▶ Unclear authority structures create confusion about decision-making.

▶ Pressure to deliver results discourages experimentation.

▶ Fear of critique leads to risk-averse behaviours, limiting innovation.

Three ways how to foster psychological safety in R&D [137]:

1. Structured problem-solving discussions: framing failures as learning opportunities encourage experimentation.

2. Aligning autonomy with clear goals: when responsibilities are well-defined, risk-taking becomes more manageable [70].

3. Encouraging open debates: constructive disagreements improve team performance and decision-making.

Without psychological safety, R&D teams risk stagnation, low collaboration, and missed breakthrough innovations [137].

Startups vs. corporations: cultural differences in psychological safety

Organizational culture significantly influences how psychological safety is fostered. Startups and large corporations present two distinct environments:

1. Startups often operate in high-speed, high-risk environments. Their flat hierarchies and flexible structures allow for fast experimentation, but this can also create instability; employees may fear that failures could impact their job security. Leaders must ensure that psychological safety exists alongside accountability, encouraging risk-taking while providing role clarity and structured feedback [138].

2. Corporations, on the other hand, offer structured decision-making, clear processes, and stability, but this can lead to a reluctance to challenge authority. Employees may fear that questioning established methods will be perceived

as insubordination. To foster psychological safety, leaders must actively encourage diverse viewpoints and challenge the status quo in a controlled, constructive way, preventing stagnation due to rigid hierarchies.

However, **both newly formed and long-standing teams can experience higher levels of psychological safety**, as new teams often rely on initial trust and group cohesion, while well-established teams benefit from strong relationships and shared norms that reinforce openness and risk-taking [115].

Balancing psychological safety across cultures means that:

▶ Startups need to reinforce stability: clear role expectations and structured feedback can make experimentation safer.

▶ Corporations must reduce fear of failure: leaders should encourage calculated risks and open discussions to avoid stagnation.

Beyond company-wide culture, sub teams within larger teams often develop their own microclimates of psychological safety. Even in corporations with rigid hierarchies, certain departments or project teams may operate with greater openness, trust, and collaboration. On the other hand, startups, despite their agility, can develop exclusive subgroups based on expertise or seniority, which may create psychological safety for some while excluding others [139].

Leaders must **ensure that psychological safety extends across the entire organization**, rather than being limited to select groups.

Psychological safety is context-dependent

Whether in remote teams, high-risk R&D environments, or structured corporate settings, the challenges of psychological safety vary, but the core principles remain the same. Teams perform at their best when employees feel safe to contribute, challenge ideas, and take risks. The key isn't just knowing that psychological safety matters, but ensuring it is adapted to the specific needs of each work environment.

Measuring and sustaining psychological safety

'Too much of a good thing'

Can there be too much psychological safety? While fostering trust and openness is essential, research suggests that excessive psychological safety when paired with low performance monitoring can lead to the 'Too-Much-of-a-Good-Thing' (TMGT) effect, where overabundant trust reduces accountability and team effectiveness [140 cited in 141]. The key is to balance psychological safety with constructive performance monitoring to ensure that teams feel safe while maintaining high standards of collaboration and innovation.

Self-assessment tools for leaders and teams

Assessing psychological safety regularly helps teams identify strengths and areas for improvement. Dr. Amy Edmondson's Psychological Safety Index (PSI) is a widely recognized tool designed to evaluate team members' perceptions of interpersonal risk-taking and their comfort in expressing ideas or concerns. Questions include:

▶ Can I bring up problems and tough issues without fear?

▶ If I make a mistake, will it be held against me?

▶ Are my contributions valued by my team?

Periodic assessments like these enable leaders to track trends, measure impact, and adjust strategies.

Key metric to track psychological safety

One of the easiest metrics of psychological safety and the one that has proven the best metric is:

▶ The error reporting rates: an increase in reported mistakes suggests that employees feel safe admitting errors without fear of retribution [97].

Conclusion: building the conditions for innovation to thrive

Psychological safety is an essential ingredient for any team striving to build innovativeness within an organization. Without it, even the most talented and diverse individuals on a team will hold back, leading to missed opportunities.

Psychological safety allows teams to unlock their full potential, as members feel comfortable sharing bold ideas, discussing them openly, learning from mistakes, and pushing boundaries together.

As a leader, creating psychological safety isn't about grand gestures. It's about what you do consistently, how you listen, how you respond, and how you create space for others to speak. What you model, you multiply.

The following takeaways and actions will help you turn this insight into daily practice, for yourself, your team, and your organization.

Key takeaways from this chapter

- ▶ Psychological safety is the foundation for innovation. It enables risk-taking, open dialogue, and learning from mistakes.

- ▶ It's not about making everyone feel comfortable all the time or avoiding accountability, it's about creating a space where people feel safe to speak up and contribute.

- ▶ Leaders play a central role in building psychological safety through behaviours like vulnerability, humility, empowerment, and integrity.

- ▶ Low psychological safety leads to silence, stagnation, and lost innovation while high safety fosters trust, creativity, and resilience.

- ▶ Effective psychological safety must be adapted to context whether in remote teams, R&D environments, or hierarchical cultures, and measured regularly to sustain impact.

Practical actions for you as a leader

To cultivate psychological safety effectively, you must move beyond theory and embed it into daily leadership practices. Here are three simple but powerful actions you could do:

1. Weekly check-in question: ask team members: 'What's one thing I could do differently as a leader to help you feel more comfortable sharing ideas?'. This encourages open feedback and signals that psychological safety is a priority.

2. Encouraging risk-taking: shift the focus from only celebrating success to rewarding experimentation. Recognize learning from failed attempts rather than just results, reinforcing that taking smart risks is valued.

3. Reinforcing a learning culture: when mistakes happen, replace blame with reflection. Instead of asking 'Who's responsible?', ask 'What did we learn? What can we do so it does not happen again?' to emphasize continuous improvement over fear of failure.

By consistently applying these small but meaningful actions, leaders can turn psychological safety from a concept into a lived experience, fostering a culture where teams feel empowered, engaged, and innovative.

Practical actions for individuals

As an individual, you play a key role in fostering psychological safety. Here are three simple but impactful actions:

1. Support each other to create a safe environment: create an environment where everyone feels heard. Acknowledge contributions, encourage open discussions, and avoid interruption. Small actions like saying 'That's an interesting perspective' build confidence and trust.

2. Give and receive feedback constructively: focus on learning, not criticism. When giving feedback, address behaviours, not personalities like 'Let's explore more options next time' instead of 'You ignored my idea.' When receiving feedback, assume positive intent and ask clarifying questions instead of reacting defensively.

3. Build trust and respect: strengthen collaboration through reliability and openness. Follow through on commitments, assume good intentions in team interactions, and respect diverse viewpoints. High-trust teams leverage differences rather than shutting them down.

By practicing these behaviours daily, you contribute to a culture of safety, trust, and open communication – making your team stronger and more innovative.

***

For additional tools related to this chapter, visit: vinco.no/future-fit-innovation-resources

PART III

ORGANIZATIONS: MANAGING THE ADDED COMPLEXITY

So far, we've explored how individuals overcome cognitive barriers like functional fixedness to unlock creativity and how teams cultivate innovation through diversity and psychological safety. But innovation doesn't stop there, it must be embedded into the very fabric of an organization.

This section shifts the focus to the organizational level, exploring two major forces shaping the future of innovation:

▶ Technological advancements: the rapid evolution of artificial intelligence (AI), automation, and digital transformation is reshaping industries. But true innovation isn't just about adopting the latest technology, it's about creating an organizational culture that embraces experimentation, adaptation, and responsible implementation.

▶ Sustainability: no longer just an ethical choice, but a business imperative. Companies that integrate sustainability into their strategies don't just comply with regulations, they future proof themselves, reduce risks, and unlock new market opportunities.

What is the link between innovation, sustainability, and technology? At first glance, sustainability and technological advancements may seem like separate challenges. One focuses on preserving resources and minimizing impact, while the other often pushes for faster growth and disruption. However, when approached strategically, they are mutually reinforcing:

▶ Sustainability drives technological progress: the need for clean energy, circular economies, and responsible production has spurred advancements in AI, material science, and automation.

▶ Technology enables sustainability: digital tools, data analytics, and AI help companies optimize resource use, reduce waste, and operate more efficiently.

▶ Organizational innovation is the connector: companies that align sustainability and technology within their culture, leadership, and structures are the ones that adapt, lead markets, and shape the future.

What is the challenge for leaders? As organizations evolve, leaders face a critical question: how can we balance sustainability and technological advancement in a way that fuels, rather than hinders, innovation?

This section explores how companies can navigate complexity, embrace change, and create environments where both sustainability and technology serve as catalysts for long-term innovation.

Let's dive in.

Chapter 6
Technology

I remember exactly where I was when I first heard the rumours: Apple was launching a 'keyboard-less' phone. It was around 2004 and at the time I was working for a telecommunications company in Croatia. I was right in the centre of the industry buzz. 'What?! How could they possibly compete with Nokia?' I thought, convinced that nothing could shake Nokia's dominance.

Back then, Nokia was *the* phone to own: an iconic, aspirational brand synonymous with quality and innovation. Nokia had been a trailblazer, launching its first internet-enabled phone in 1996 and becoming the world's largest phone manufacturer by 1998 [142]. Yet despite this strong market position, Apple ruined its dominance. Nokia failed to recognize the seismic shift that the iPhone would bring. The reasons for Nokia's downfall are multifaceted: resistance to change, a misplaced focus on hardware over software, ineffective marketing and collaboration strategies, and leadership missteps, including an overreliance on its brand's goodwill and legacy value.

Fast forward to today, and history is repeating itself. In early 2025, DeepSeek entered the AI race, shaking the dominance of U.S. tech giants. The market reacted instantly: tech stocks tumbled; analysts scrambled. But why was anyone surprised? With China's relentless tech advancements, hundreds of patents filed, this moment was inevitable.

Time will tell how resistant U.S. AI giants will be to Chinese competition. However, in this battle for AI dominance, Europe remains largely silent. Why? Because innovation isn't driven by technology alone – it requires the right mindset, adaptive business models, a robust investment culture geared toward scale [143], and ideally, a coherent market to accelerate growth. Europe is technologically capable, but it has been slower to mobilize these enablers at scale in the AI race; partly due to the complexity of operating across 27 countries, and partly because of the challenging patent landscape that new entrants must navigate. These are real obstacles, but they're not excuses. If Europe wants to compete, they need to stop romanticizing the narrative and start putting this goal clearly on the agenda.

Both Nokia and U.S. tech giants share a common blind spot: they were, or are, fixated on their market dominance, anchored to past successes, believing those will guarantee future growth. But history shows us that clinging to what worked before is often what leads to failure. True innovation isn't about protecting the past, it's about continuously adapting to an uncertain future. The same applies not just to companies, but to individuals and teams who resist change.

This pattern of technological disruption is nothing new. Those who cling to past successes risk being overtaken by those who embrace change.

Technology has profoundly transformed our lives in ways that often surpass our full comprehension. The ability to send a message across the globe instantaneously or access vast amounts of information from nearly any location in seconds has fundamentally reshaped how we live, work, and connect with the world. These advancements didn't emerge overnight; they are the culmination of centuries of progress, with each breakthrough building upon the last; from the invention of the wheel to today's James Webb Space Telescope.

This cumulative innovation, where past discoveries lay the groundwork for new developments, has brought us to our current technological stage and will continue to drive progress. However, as technology advances at an unprecedented pace, it often ventures into the 'unimaginable', posing challenges for individuals and organizations to fully grasp or accept its potential. This resistance stems from a fixation on the familiar, which creates barriers to envisioning how new technologies can reshape habits, lifestyles, and, ultimately, entire industries and markets.

So, what determines whether companies, leaders, and teams successfully adapt to technological change? What separates those who embrace the future from those who resist it?

The answer lies in how we combine and leverage technological advancements. Emerging technologies enable innovative ways of integrating various resources, physical, human, digital, data, and financial, leading to new efficiencies, products, and services [144]. They don't just change industries; they fuel entrepreneurial activity, acting as catalysts for both process, product [144] and service innovation.

And yet, not all organizations succeed in integrating technology. Some thrive, while others fade into irrelevance. Why? **Because successful technological transformation isn't just about having access to new tools, it's about people.** It is individuals, employees, leaders, and teams, who shape organizations, and it is their mindset and actions that determine whether technology becomes an enabler of progress or a missed opportunity. Have a look at the case on Sparebanken Norge at the end of this chapter, it illustrates how a 200-year-old bank leverages technology and culture to stay future-fit.

In this chapter we will take a closer look at:

- ▶ What drives technological change and how it fuels innovation across industries.

- ▶ The psychological, structural, and strategic barriers that prevent effective technology adoption.

▶ How leaders can navigate these barriers and foster a culture that embraces experimentation and learning.

▶ Why digital transformation must align with strategic goals – not just efficiency, but also sustainability.

▶ How to ensure that technology adoption becomes a long-term driver of value and sustainability, not a source of resistance.

By the end of this chapter, you'll understand how to lead technological change with purpose: building a culture where innovation takes root and sustainability guides progress.

The role of technology in innovation

Technology as the engine of innovation

The impact of technology on economic growth has been undeniable. Between 2013 and 2023, the ICT sector grew three times faster than the total economy across 27 OECD countries [145]. Investment in generative AI surged from USD 1.3 billion in 2022 to USD 17.8 billion in 2023, while the number of IoT devices is expected to increase 2.5 times from 2023 levels, reaching 39 billion by 2029 [145]. Moreover, AI serves as a driver of productivity and economic growth by increasing efficiency and improving decision-making processes [146]. In medicine, AI accelerates the identification of potential drug candidates, optimizes preclinical and clinical testing, and reduces costs, thereby expediting the development of new cancer therapies [147].

Digital transformation has integrated technology deeply into business operations and consumer lifestyles, making it a central driver of global innovation and economy.

How technology creates innovation

Technology drives innovation through two main channels: increasing efficiencies and creating opportunities [148].

Increasing efficiencies involves optimizing internal processes, making them faster, cheaper, and more scalable. By streamlining operations, reducing costs, and improving accuracy, companies can significantly enhance their performance without substantially altering the customer experience [148]. For example, smart contracts in blockchain remove intermediaries, reducing transaction costs. Cloud computing has enabled businesses to scale operations instantly, reducing infrastructure expenses and increasing flexibility. AI-powered predictive models optimize supply chains by calculating the most efficient shipping pathways.

Creating new opportunities means transforming how businesses interact with customers, capture their needs, and even redefine entire industries. In other words, creating new opportunities means expanding customer reach, better addressing their needs, or enabling entirely new business models that weren't possible before [148]. Subscription-based platforms (Netflix, Spotify) emerged by leveraging AI-driven personalization and cloud computing. Blockchain-based decentralized finance (DeFi) challenged traditional banking by enabling peer-to-peer transactions without intermediaries. AI-driven diagnostics allow early disease detection, reducing the burden on hospitals and improving patient outcomes [148].

How technology transforms business models

Beyond efficiency and opportunity, technology fundamentally reshapes business models. **Organizations use digital tools not just to optimize operations but to redefine how they create, deliver, and capture value:**

▶ Value creation – enabling new products, services, and networks: technology allows companies to develop new products, redefine customer engagement, and create value across digital networks [149]. For example, by integrating AI, automation, and IoT, businesses now leverage data analytics to personalize services and anticipate customer needs, making products more adaptive and responsive.

Digital channels enhance customer engagement and improve decision-making through real-time insights and predictive analytics. Blockchain-based systems provide security and transparency, increasing customer trust.

▶ Value delivery – how businesses use technology to operate: value delivery refers to how businesses integrate technology into their operations to improve efficiency and customer experience. Technology, however, also enhances company's internal capabilities [150]. To effectively deliver value for its customers, business need to update their operations and develop scalable, modular platforms [150]. As digital eco-system are becoming more comprehensive, they reshape roles and responsibilities within industrial ecosystems [150].

▶ Value capture – transforming revenue models: value capture focuses on ensuring financial sustainability by generating new or increased revenue streams and optimizing cost structures [150]. Digital technologies facilitate this by enabling innovative revenue models such as subscriptions and pay-per-use, which offer flexible, real-time pricing based on operational data. Emerging technologies like blockchain further enhance value capture by providing transparency and fostering trust among stakeholders [150].

The hidden challenge: technology alone isn't enough

Yet, despite the incredible opportunities that digitalization and emerging technologies provide, many companies struggle to keep up. The challenge isn't just about having access to AI, blockchain, or cloud computing; it's about the ability to integrate these technologies effectively.

True digital transformation requires more than investment; it demands a fundamental shift in mindset, leadership, and organizational adaptability. Companies that fail to evolve often suffer from rigid structures, outdated processes, and resistance to change ultimately preventing innovation from taking root.

Why do so many organizations struggle with technological adoption and, more importantly, what you as a leader can do to overcome these barriers and drive real innovation?

Resistance to technology adoption: why companies struggle to innovate

Technological advancements are a powerful driver of innovation, often reshaping behaviours, processes, and entire industries. But with change comes uncertainty and organizations often struggle to keep pace.

For innovation to succeed, it must first be embraced from within. Adoption starts at the top – leaders must champion new technology, secure internal buy-in, and align innovation with strategic goals to ensure meaningful impact. Without this foundation, resistance emerges, slowing progress and creating barriers to transformation.

The biggest barriers are not technological, they are psychological, structural, and strategic. Leaders often assume that acquiring new technology is enough, but without the right mindset and approach, adoption stalls.

Psychological barriers to technology adoption: individuals

Resistance to technological advancements is often how individuals react to change. We naturally prefer stability, and when innovation disrupts familiar processes, it triggers psychological resistance [151]. Oreg (2003) identifies six key psychological barriers that hinder technology adoption [152]:

1. Fear of losing control or becoming obsolete: new technology can change roles and responsibilities, making employees feel they have less influence over their work or worry that their skills will no longer be relevant or valued. This often leads to defensive behaviours and skepticism toward change. In some cases, these fears have been justified, as organizations have used technology to cut costs by reducing headcount rather than reskilling workers.

Example: in customer service, employees have resisted AI-powered tools not because they question their efficiency, but because they fear being sidelined. Yet, in well-managed cases, AI is used to support decision-making, not replace it, allowing professionals to do their jobs with more insight and less administrative burden.

2. Cognitive rigidity: some individuals resist new technologies simply because they are stuck in old ways of thinking. Dogmatism or a stubborn unwillingness to consider alternative approaches can prevent people from recognizing the benefits of innovation.

Example: Kodak dismissed digital photography because it was too attached to its film business, ultimately leading to its downfall.

3. Lack of psychological resilience: technology adoption requires adaptation, which some individuals find stressful. Those with lower psychological resilience struggle with uncertainty, making them more likely to reject change.

Example: employees in traditional industries often resist automation tools because they fear it will lead to job losses.

4. Intolerance for the adjustment period: even when technology provides long-term benefits, the short-term effort required to learn and adapt can be a barrier. Many people prefer to stick with familiar workflows rather than endure temporary discomfort.

Example: companies implementing enterprise resource planning (ERP) systems often face resistance due to the complexity of transitioning from older systems.

5. Preference for stability: some individuals inherently prefer low-stimulation environments, making them less receptive to novelty. When technology introduces too many changes at once, it can feel overwhelming.

Example: older employees may struggle with cloud-based collaboration tools after years of using local data storage and traditional email communication. However, COVID-19 showed us that when there is urgency, we all find ways to adapt and accept digital solutions almost instantly.

6. Habitual resistance to change: people build deeply ingrained habits around familiar technologies. When those habits are disrupted, it can feel uncomfortable or even stressful, making them associate the new technology with frustration rather than improvement.

Example: many professionals resisted transitioning from physical documents to digital records due to years of paper-based workflows. I, for example, love paper books and resist switching to Kindle or audio books.

Psychological barriers to technology adoption: organizations

While psychological resistance is often most visible at the individual level, the same behavioural patterns can manifest at an organizational scale because, ultimately, organizations are made up of individuals whose mindsets, fears, and habits shape the broader culture. When enough individuals share the same concerns or uncertainties, those attitudes become embedded in team dynamics, decision-making processes, and eventually, in institutional behaviour [151].

In these cases, resistance is no longer just about individuals, it becomes systemic. Organizations may collectively hesitate to implement new tools due to perceived risks, unclear benefits, or attachment to familiar routines and vendor relationships [151].

As an example, autonomous vehicles face widespread resistance not only from individual users, but also from entire industries and regulatory bodies, due to concerns around safety, accountability, and public trust.

Case study: barriers to adoption of autonomous vehicles

Autonomous vehicles (AVs) showcase AI's potential to transform transportation, using machine learning, sensor data, and real-time decision-making to navigate roads, avoid obstacles, and operate without human input. In theory, AVs could enhance mobility, optimize logistics, and reduce accidents caused by human error.

Many of my peers, including myself, often say that we become part-time taxi drivers after work: shuttling their kids to and from after-school activities. Imagine a world where self-driving cars take over routine tasks: picking up our children from school or delivering goods 24/7? How much time could we save, and free up for other activities, instead of spending it driving? In logistics, autonomous trucks could reduce delivery times and reshape supply chains, operating at night when roads are less congested.

However, despite these advantages, AV technology remains stuck in the testing phase, facing significant psychological, regulatory, and structural barriers. According to Raj et al. (2020), these key factors hinder AV adoption [153]:

1. Security and privacy concerns: AVs generate vast amounts of user data, raising concerns about data security and surveillance.

2. Lack of public trust: many people remain skeptical of driverless cars, fearing malfunctions and safety risks.

3. Obscurity in accountability: it remains unclear who is responsible for AV-related accidents: the manufacturer, owner, or software provider.

4. High costs and social inequality: AVs are expensive, making them inaccessible to lower-income groups and potentially widening economic divides.

5. Infrastructure challenges: roads, traffic systems, and urban layouts require significant upgrades to accommodate AVs.

6. Regulatory and standardization gaps: A lack of global safety standards and regulations slows development and public acceptance.

7. Job displacement fears: AVs threaten jobs in trucking, taxi services, and delivery industries, leading to social and political resistance.

The study also showed that fear of riding in an autonomous vehicle is the biggest barrier to adoption [153]. An EU study confirms that widespread discomfort and trust issues are major obstacles [154]. Addressing these challenges requires coordinated efforts from governments, policymakers, and industry leaders to develop clear regulations, enhance security measures, and build public confidence.

This study reinforces a key theme from the section: **resistance to technology adoption is not purely a technical issue, it's deeply psychological, regulatory, and structural.** AVs, like many emerging technologies, face public skepticism, unclear governance, and high implementation costs – barriers that slow down adoption even when the technology itself is ready.

Organizational barriers to technology adoption

While individual resistance plays a significant role in slowing down technological adoption, structural and strategic obstacles within organizations often present even greater roadblocks to technology adoption. Companies may acknowledge the importance of new technologies, but struggle to integrate them due to structural inefficiencies, outdated leadership strategies, or internal resistance to transformation.

Moreover, the most common organizational barriers include:

▶ Rigid corporate structures, costs, and bureaucracy: large organizations, particularly in the public sector, often have complex decision-making hierarchies, which slow down the adoption of new technologies. Even when technology is acknowledged as valuable, a lack of clear strategy, resources for training, and structured implementation can prevent widespread adoption.

Example: AI has entered workplaces on a large scale, yet many public institutions struggle with structured adoption. While some universities and government organizations have granted employees access to ChatGPT through shared platforms, they have not developed a clear AI strategy or provided structured education on its use. Departments and individuals have not received tailored guidance on how AI could benefit their specific needs, and there has been no survey to assess which employees are advanced users versus those who are falling behind. As a result, only a handful of eager individuals experiment with tools and expand their exploration, while the majority remain hesitant or avoid AI altogether [86].

Additionally, training an entire organization on AI would require significant resources. Reskilling comes at a cost. Assessments, tailored training, and support programs all require financial and strategic commitment, a cost that not all organizations are willing to take on.

This highlights a common challenge in large institutions: **while the technology is available, a lack of structured implementation, training, and leadership support creates an uneven adoption process.**

In contrast, private-sector companies with more agile structures have successfully integrated AI by prioritizing structured training and leadership-driven adoption strategies. For example, some smaller Norwegian tech companies have implemented AI onboarding programs that assess employees' skill levels, provide tailored AI education, and designate AI ambassadors within teams to support adoption [86]. By proactively addressing knowledge gaps and embedding AI into workflows, these companies ensure that AI adoption is strategic, structured, and company-wide, rather than leaving employees to figure it out on their own.

▶ Short-term focus vs. long-term investment: many organizations prioritize immediate cost-cutting over long-term innovation, viewing technology adoption as an expense rather than an investment.

Example: some hospitals might hesitate to adopt AI-based diagnostics due to the high upfront costs, despite long-term efficiency gains.

▶ Leadership resistance and risk aversion: executives may be hesitant to take risks on emerging technology, fearing failure or disrupting existing revenue streams.

Example: Nokia's leadership failed to anticipate the smartphone revolution, despite internal warnings, because they prioritized protecting their existing market share.

▶ Regulatory and compliance constraints: some industries face strict legal and compliance challenges that prevent them from rapidly integrating new technologies.

Example: the financial sector faces hurdles in adopting blockchain due to unclear regulations and compliance risks.

Even the most advanced technology will fail without the right organizational foundation. To move beyond resistance and drive real transformation, leaders must take active steps to reshape company structures, foster adaptability, and embed innovation into daily operations. In the next section, we explore strategic leadership actions that can help organizations overcome these barriers and turn technology into a driver of long-term success.

Theoretical models explaining resistance

Resistance to technology adoption is a complex phenomenon influenced by both individual behaviour and organizational dynamics. Several well-established models help explain why resistance occurs and how organizations can address it.

Rogers' diffusion of innovations theory

Rogers' (1971) framework segments people into the following categories based on their willingness to adopt new technology [155]:

1. Laggards: the most resistant, typically older individuals deeply rooted in tradition. They often have limited financial resources, smaller social networks, and little influence on broader societal trends.

2. Innovators: the first to adopt new technologies, usually younger, financially stable, and well-connected within scientific and innovation communities. Their openness to risk allows them to embrace new technologies early, even when the likelihood of failure is high.

3. Early adopters, early majority, and late majority: these groups represent varying degrees of openness to technological change, with adoption increasing as the technology becomes more widespread and accessible.

To successfully drive technology adoption, leaders must identify who the innovators and laggards are within their organizations. Innovators should be leveraged as allies. Enabling innovators to experiment and grow their enthusiasm will turn them into ambassadors for technological advancements acceptance, helping and persuading more skeptical employees to overcome fear and start to experiment themselves.

Example: electric vehicles followed this model, early adopters embraced them for environmental benefits, and their higher social status and financial stability allowed them to experiment with the technology. However, the late majority only adopted EVs when charging infrastructure improved and government subsidies made them more affordable.

Innovation resistance theory (IRT)

Ram and Sheth (1989) define innovation resistance as the tendency to reject new technologies to preserve the status quo.

This resistance falls into two categories: functional barriers and psychological barriers [151].

1. Functional barriers: occur when an innovation does not meet user needs or creates adoption challenges [151]:

   ▶ Value barrier: no clear advantage over existing solutions (e.g., blockchain initially struggled due to unclear benefits).

   ▶ Complexity barrier: difficult to understand or use (e.g., early AI tools were seen as too technical).

   ▶ Compatibility barrier: does not align with existing products or habits (e.g., EV adoption lagged due to lack of charging stations).

   ▶ Risk barrier: perceived financial, security, or functional risks (e.g., autonomous vehicles face safety concerns).

2. Psychological barriers: arise when technology conflicts with social norms or behaviours [151]:

   ▶ Norm barrier: contradicts industry culture (e.g., remote work met resistance before COVID-19).

   ▶ Image barrier: negative brand or country associations (e.g., concerns over Chinese 5G technology).

   ▶ Information barrier: unclear communication fuels uncertainty (e.g., AI privacy concerns in HR).

Understanding these barriers helps leaders develop targeted strategies to overcome resistance and drive successful technology adoption.

Upper Echelons Theory

The Upper Echelons Theory suggests that organizational decisions and innovation strategies are shaped by top leadership [156]. Leaders influence strategic direction, resource allocation, and the speed at which new technologies are embraced [157].

A leader's personal risk tolerance, openness to change, and perception of innovation often dictate whether their organization adapts quickly or falls behind. Those with an 'Innovator' mindset proactively seek out emerging technologies and cultivate a culture of experimentation, while those with a 'Laggard' mindset may resist change, delaying adoption and creating structural roadblocks.

Example: some Nokia managers reportedly recognized the disruptive potential of the iPhone early on but struggled to convince top decision-makers to act. The leadership's overconfidence in existing market dominance and reluctance to pivot resulted in missed opportunities, ultimately leading to Nokia's decline [158]. This case highlights how leadership inertia can have severe long-term consequences, not just for a company, but for entire industries.

To drive innovation, leaders must be willing to challenge the status quo, make bold strategic shifts, and foster an environment where technology adoption is seen as a long-term investment rather than a risk. Without visionary leadership, even the most advanced technologies will struggle to gain traction.

What does this mean for you as a leader?

Each of these theories offers a unique perspective on why resistance occurs whether at the individual, organizational, or leadership level.

As a leader, understanding these models allows you to anticipate resistance, develop targeted adoption strategies, and foster a culture where technology adoption happens naturally rather than through force or compliance.

So, how can you as a leader take proactive steps to overcome resistance and drive sustainable innovation adoption?

How leaders can overcome resistance and foster a tech-positive culture

Technology adoption is not just about having the right tools, it's about creating an environment where innovation thrives. As a leader, your first step is to recognize your own stance: are you an innovator who embraces change, or a laggard who hesitates? Next, assess the state of technology adoption within your team or organization: what barriers exist, and where is resistance coming from?

Once you identify these obstacles, your role is to act decisively breaking down resistance, build trust in technology, and fostering a culture where employees feel empowered to embrace change rather than fear it.

Five steps that can guide you in overcoming resistance

1. Lead by example: demonstrate openness
People look to leadership for cues on how to respond to change. If leaders hesitate or show skepticism, employees will mirror that resistance.

What you can do:

▷ Be an active user of emerging technologies – experiment with AI tools, automation, or digital platforms.

▷ Share success stories and failures and learnings from within and outside the organization to demonstrate real-world impact.

▷ Encourage a learning mindset, showing that even leaders are adapting to new technology.

Example: when Satya Nadella took over as CEO of Microsoft, he made cloud computing and AI a priority, using the technology himself and championing a growth mindset across the company. The result? Microsoft transformed from a slow-moving giant into an innovation leader [159].

2. Create a safe environment for experimentation
Many employees resist technology because they fear making mistakes or being replaced. As we explored in earlier chapters, psychological safety is essential, without it, innovation stalls.

Leaders must foster an environment where adopting new technology is seen as an opportunity for growth, not a threat to job security.

What you can do:

▶ Encourage experimentation – allow teams to test new tools without fear of failure.

▶ Reward curiosity and initiative rather than focusing only on results.

▶ Frame technology adoption as a way to enhance roles, not eliminate them.

Example: Google's '20% time policy' allowed employees to dedicate time to innovation, leading to breakthroughs like Gmail and Google Maps. By creating a low-risk environment for trying new ideas, employees felt encouraged to explore technology.

3. Invest in digital skills and training
Access to technology is meaningless if employees don't know how to use it effectively. Many organizations fail to adopt innovation simply because they don't invest in digital upskilling.

What you can do:

▶ Identify tech skill gaps within teams and offer targeted training.

▶ Appoint digital champions; internal experts who help others adopt new tools.

▶ Make training ongoing, not a one-time initiative.

Example: training doesn't have to be costly or time-consuming. A simple yet effective approach is to create short, 30-minute educational videos tailored to different levels of technological competence. This makes learning accessible, practical, and easy to integrate into daily work. Many social media influencers successfully build their audiences' skills using this exact approach – delivering bite-sized, engaging content that drives continuous learning.

This is particularly important when adopting advanced technologies like AI, which can't simply be 'plugged in'. They require a thoughtful, phased approach to adoption, both technically and culturally.

Additional takeaways on AI adoption: to successfully integrate AI into innovation management, leaders must go beyond simply adopting new tools. AI adoption requires a strategic approach, cultural readiness, and organizational alignment. Here are three key steps to foster AI-driven innovation in your company [160]:

1. AI- based innovation management requires substantial technical and organizational changes to cope with the associated challenges. Group comparisons revealed that AI-innovators vary in the implementation challenges they face, such as insufficient access to data or a lack of technical expertise.

2. AI-based innovation management cannot be implemented with a one-size-fits-all approach. Organizations clearly differ in their preferences of how they may use and implement AI-based innovation management.

3. AI-based innovation management needs adequate implementation to tap full potential. AI implementation managers must ensure that major internal stakeholders and external partners are aligned and compliant with the AI-based innovation management goals.

While AI enhances efficiency, employees are far more likely to embrace it when they understand how it improves the quality of their work, supports better decisions, and expands their impact, not just as a cost-cutting tool. To drive meaningful adoption, leaders must position AI as an enabler of higher productivity, creativity, and value creation, not merely automation.

4. Align technology adoption with strategic goals
Technology and innovation should never feel like a disconnected initiative, it should be clearly tied to business objectives, so employees see its purpose.

What you can do:

- ▶ Show how technology improves efficiency, collaboration, and customer experience.

- ▶ Set clear goals for tech adoption with measurable outcomes.

- ▶ Link technology initiatives to company values, if sustainability is a focus, highlight how digital transformation contributes.

Example: a global logistics company struggling with warehouse automation reframed technology adoption to improve worker safety, reduce waste, and increase efficiency. This helped employees view automation as an enhancement, not a disruption.

5. Build a culture of continuous learning and adaptability
The pace of technological change means that stagnation is not an option. Leaders must embed adaptability into company culture, ensuring employees stay future-ready.

What you can do:

- ▶ Shift from a fixed mindset ('we've always done it this way') to a growth mindset ('let's find a better way').

- ▶ Encourage cross-functional collaboration so employees gain exposure to new technologies.

- ▶ Regularly evaluate emerging trends and adjust strategies accordingly.

Example: Netflix has maintained its dominance by constantly adapting to new technologies, from DVD rentals to streaming to AI-driven recommendations. This wasn't just a technological shift; it was a cultural shift toward innovation.

Leaders set the tone not only for psychological safety but also for technology. By fostering openness, safety, skills development, alignment with strategy, and a culture of adaptability, organizations can transform resistance into momentum.

Technology adoption isn't just about rolling out new systems, it's about shaping a culture where employees feel confident, engaged, and empowered to innovate. In the next section, we explore how digital transformation intersects with sustainability and why integrating technology with environmental responsibility is key to long-term business success.

The impact of technology on sustainability: challenges and opportunities

Technology and digital transformation have become essential drivers of economic growth, innovation, and efficiency. However, these advancements also come with significant sustainability challenges. The increasing reliance on digital technologies has deep environmental consequences, including high energy consumption, resource depletion, and electronic waste. As leaders push for innovation, they must also recognize their responsibility to integrate sustainability into technology adoption.

The environmental cost of digitalization

While the digital economy fuels global progress, it also exacerbates sustainability concerns [161]:

▶ Resource dependency: the production of digital devices requires critical minerals and vast amounts of raw materials, contributing to environmental degradation. Manufacturing a two-kilogram computer requires approximately 800 kilograms of raw materials, highlighting the intensity of resource use.

▶ Energy consumption and emissions: the ICT sector accounts for 6% to 12% of global electricity use, with emissions from data centres, blockchain, AI, and IoT increasing annually. In 2022, data centres consumed 460 terawatt-hours (TWh); equivalent to the energy consumption of France. The growing energy demands of digital infrastructure require urgent action to improve efficiency. Investing in low-energy computing, optimized logistics, and AI-driven energy solutions can help significantly reduce emissions.

▶ Digital waste and environmental inequities: e-waste is the fastest-growing waste stream, yet only 7.5% of digital waste in developing countries is formally collected, compared to 47% in developed nations. This disparity leaves developing nations to manage hazardous, low-value waste while valuable components are exported elsewhere.

Technology as a sustainability enabler

Despite the sustainability challenges associated with digitalization, technology also provides solutions when applied strategically. Businesses that integrate sustainability into their innovation strategies can reduce environmental impact while unlocking new efficiencies and business models.

One key approach is the circular economy and sustainable product design. To reduce digital waste and extend product life cycles, companies must focus on repairable, recyclable, and upgradeable products. Transitioning to a circular economy, where resources are continuously repurposed, can significantly minimize environmental impact.

Example: some companies are already redesigning their products with sustainability in mind. Fairphone, for instance, produces modular smartphones that allow users to replace and upgrade individual components, reducing electronic waste and promoting responsible consumerism.

But sustainable innovation isn't just about how products are made, it's also about how value is delivered. Business models themselves can be redesigned to align with both environmental and social goals.

For example, the NHS in England is piloting a 'Netflix-style' subscription model to drive antibiotic innovation. Developing antibiotics for resistant bacteria is costly, yet these drugs are rarely used because they are reserved for exceptional cases, making the traditional sales model commercially unviable. With the subscription model, the government pays a fixed fee for access, ensuring availability when needed while providing pharmaceutical companies with a predictable revenue stream [162].

This is a powerful example of how an innovative business model, inspired by the tech industry, can be adapted to meet long-term public health needs while also supporting sustainable innovation.

Conclusion: technology, leadership and the path forward

Technology has always been a powerful driver of innovation, reshaping industries and creating new opportunities. Yet, as this chapter has shown, adopting technology successfully requires more than just access to new tools, it demands the right leadership, a culture of adaptability, and a strategy for overcoming resistance.

Key takeaways from this chapter

- ▶ Technology drives innovation, but people determine its success. Leadership, employees, and organizational structures either accelerate or block adoption.

- ▶ Resistance is natural but not inevitable. Understanding why people resist, whether due to psychological, organizational, or leadership barriers, helps develop better adoption strategies.

▶ Successful leaders foster a tech-positive culture. They invest in digital skills, encourage experimentation, and align technology with strategic business goals.

▶ Sustainability is the next frontier. Technology adoption must now consider environmental impact, ensuring innovation is not just fast and efficient, but also sustainable.

Looking ahead: technology and sustainability

Technology adoption is no longer just about efficiency or competitive advantage, it must also be sustainable. Organizations that integrate innovation with environmental responsibility will not only reduce their ecological footprint but also drive long-term business success. The next chapter explores sustainability and how it interacts with technology. But before that let's look at a real-life case, Sparebanken Norge, how it transformed into a tech-forward bank through a deep cultural shift.

Case study: Sparebanken Norge – building culture, technology, and trust together

When a company is over 200 years old, you might expect it to be slow, cautious, and resistant to change. But Sparebanken Norge (shortened SBN, until spring 2025 known as Sparebanken Vest), headquartered in Bergen and operating across western Norway, proves that tradition and transformation are not mutually exclusive. The bank has managed to blend its deep community roots with forward-leaning innovation, using culture, technology, and collective learning as the foundation.

I spoke with Siren Sundland, Executive Vice President of Technology and Business Processes, about how SBN is building a future-fit bank, not through top-down mandates, but through a culture that embraces trust, learning, and shared responsibility.

A bank owned by its people – and powered by culture

Sparebanken Norge is not like most banks. The organization's model of *samfunnseierskap* – social ownership – is more than an equity structure. It's a mindset. The bank's goal is for 60% ownership to remain with customers and local communities. That sense of shared purpose underpins how the bank approaches both its business and its internal operations [163].

As Siren shared, 'Collaboration and learning culture is at the core of what we do.' It's not just words. It's a strategy. Over the years, SBN has gone through transformations, and internal restructuring, all with a clear focus: to learn faster than the competition and to change behaviour from the inside out [163].

They began by asking a fundamental question: 'What do we want to stand for while fighting to build the bank? Not values on posters, but concrete, visible behaviour' [163].

The answer was: **Team play.**

SBN had recognized challenges many mature organizations face; siloed thinking, unproductive internal competition, and a lack of shared respect across departments, teams talked behind each other's backs. There was little cross-unit collaboration or willingness to challenge status quo. Leaders knew that breaking this cycle required more than one-off workshops. It required a culture shift [163].

Turning culture into measurable behaviour

The leadership team translated 'team play' into concrete, observable behaviours. Directors were required to speak positively about peers, both in public and behind closed doors. Employees were encouraged to lift up colleagues not just in their own teams, but in entirely different parts of the organization. These new expectations were not left to interpretation; they became part of evaluation, salary, and bonus structures [163].

This was the bank's way of **making psychological safety real.** Not just something talked about in leadership programs, but **a behaviourally anchored goal across the business.**

Learning from friction, not avoiding it

One of the most insightful parts of our conversation was Siren's view on conflict and disagreement. 'Friction isn't something to avoid', she said. 'It's a natural part of growth. What matters is that we're not afraid of it and that we know how to work through it.' [163]

She described how SBN, like any large organization, has to continuously balance tradition and change. 'We'll never fully solve the question of who we are as a bank', she added. 'Our challenge is to preserve our core while stimulating progress' [163]. That balance shows up in how they use **technology, not to replace relationships, but to enhance them.**

SBN is a bank that highly values local branches and customer-facing advisors. But it's also a bank that builds cutting-edge credit processes, where AI and data analytics support advisors by eliminating the administrative burden allowing them to focus on human relationships. Technology is seen as an enabler, a strength and not a threat [163].

And how do employees react to these shifts? By focusing on learning [163].

SBN has cultivated a culture where employees are not just permitted, but encouraged to try, experiment, and learn. One of the key messages from CEO Jan Erik Kjerpeseth is: **Mistakes happen. Own them. Learn from them. Move on.** No blame. No fear. That's psychological safety in action [163].

Integrating technology without losing the human side

SPV's recent consolidation with Sparebanken Sør and rebranding to Sparebanken Norge has introduced new challenges. Two headquarters. Two cultures. Different levels of technical maturity [163].

Rather than focus on technical tools alone, SPV is building **interdisciplinary teams** and designing a strategic **onboarding program** to ensure strong continuation of knowledge sharing and learning loops. The goal isn't just integration, it's growth. As Siren explained, 'We're not just trying to align systems. We're trying to get the best from both banks. That starts with culture and people' [163].

The bank's innovation doesn't stop when new systems go live. It continues. Projects are launched, improved, optimized, and learned from. That mindset, that **innovation is iterative**, is embedded in how SBN operates [163].

Psychological safety as a performance strategy

What struck me most was how deliberate SBN is about building a safe, high-performance culture. Leadership development programs like Handlekraft equip leaders across Western Norway, not just within SBN, with tools to lead through uncertainty. Internally, feedback and trust-building are practiced through arenas where employees share learnings openly. 'The more stories we share,' Siren noted, 'the more people feel comfortable doing the same' [163].

And results follow. In the past three years, SBN has consistently ranked the top-performing bank in Norway. For them, **innovation isn't just about new products, it's about how people behave** [163].

Siren summed it up perfectly: 'Innovation is about using what we know to create something new and useful.' At SBN, knowledge isn't locked in systems, it's shared in conversations, teams, and across disciplines [163].

Lessons for leaders

The Sparebanken Norge story offers a model for any organization navigating change. The banking industry is undergoing significant transformation, with technological advancements as one of the most crucial enablers. However, Sparebanken Norge understands that technology is just a tool; it's the people and how they interact that form the true core of innovation.

Innovation doesn't start with tools. It starts with trust. With clear expectations. With team play. And with leaders who walk the talk.

What SPV teaches us

▶ Innovation must be grounded in culture, not just structure or systems.

▶ Psychological safety is measurable and actionable, not abstract.

▶ Technology should free up human capacity, not replace it.

▶ Learning is a leadership responsibility and a competitive strategy.

In the end, Sparebanken Norge is proof that a 200-year-old bank can be one of the most future-fit organizations around, not by chasing trends, but by building a culture where people, technology, and shared purpose move forward together simultaneously giving back to society and strengthening the regional ecosystem.[1]

**

For additional tools related to this chapter, visit: vinco.no/future-fit-innovation-resources

---

[1] This case study was developed independently. I have no financial ties to Sparebanken Norge, nor was I compensated for including them in this book.

Chapter 7
Sustainability

Imagine this: you're a medium-sized company, a subcontractor for a larger one, and business has been steady. Then, without warning, your biggest client cancels your contract. Confused, you ask why. Their response: 'Your company doesn't have an ESG (Environmental, Social, and Governance) strategy.'

Your leadership team is in shock. You're not a multinational corporation. You don't fall under mandatory reporting requirements. Sustainability always seemed like a big company's concern. But suddenly, it's clear: sustainability isn't just about regulations, it's about staying in business.

Now imagine a different scenario. Your company is thriving, until a major supply chain disruption hits, triggered by extreme weather. Costs skyrocket, deliveries stall, and customers grow frustrated. You scramble to fix the issue, but the damage is already done.

This happened to us at Vinco.

In the fall of 2023, we hired new employees and ordered new PCs. But then storm Hans hit eastern Norway. Flooding and landslides brought train lines between Bergen and Oslo to a halt. The warehouse where our PCs were being delivered from was completely flooded. Customer service was unreachable. Days passed. Weeks. Our new hires were waiting for equipment that simply wasn't coming. I was frustrated. In the end, the whole order had to be cancelled and restarted. It took nearly two months to get those PCs.

Now imagine another retail company that also sells PCs, but this company has embedded sustainability into its strategy. They've anticipated supply chain disruptions. They've diversified their logistics. They've built resilience into their operations. While others scramble, they adapt and turn disruption into opportunity.

Sustainability isn't just about meeting regulations. It's a strategic driver of innovation, resilience, and long-term growth.
In this chapter, I'll explore how businesses can move beyond compliance and leverage sustainability as a competitive advantage.

Let's unpack the key ideas I am covering in this chapter:

▶ Why sustainability is no longer optional, but a strategic driver of innovation, resilience, and long-term growth.

▶ The evolving role of sustainability in business, from compliance to competitive advantage.

▶ The most common barriers to sustainable innovation and how regulations, consumers, and markets are shifting the landscape.

▶ How sustainability pressures are reshaping business models, creating opportunities for circularity, efficiency, and new revenue streams.

▶ Real-world strategies and leadership lessons from companies like BIR AS that are embedding sustainability into innovation culture.

▶ Five practical steps leaders can take to align sustainability with strategy and activate real change within their teams and organizations.

By the end of this chapter, you'll understand why sustainability is not a burden or barrier, but a source of competitive advantage and how you can start to harness it to drive innovation, strengthen resilience, and create lasting value for your business.

Sustainability: a strategic imperative

At its core, sustainability means creating systems that meet society's long-term needs while respecting the planet's ecological limits. But today, voluntary efforts are no longer enough. Environmental degradation and climate risks have reached a tipping point, pushing governments and global institutions to implement mandatory sustainability measures. What was once a strategic option is now a business necessity; a prerequisite for market participation, resilience, and long-term success.

Sustainability is built on three interconnected pillars:

1. Economic sustainability ensures long-term business growth while considering societal and environmental impact.

2. Environmental sustainability focuses on responsible resource use, ecosystem protection, and climate action.

3. Social sustainability prioritizes equity, inclusion, and human rights, fostering fair opportunities for all. (Some of which I covered in the Part II.)

Balancing these pillars isn't easy, but companies that do, gain a competitive edge. While **integrating sustainability into operations presents challenges like higher costs, compliance burdens, and strategic shifts, it also unlocks opportunities.**

A strong sustainability culture, one that values diversity, psychological safety, and innovation, drives creativity, resilience, and long-term growth. Companies that embed sustainability into their governance and innovation frameworks are better positioned to anticipate risks, adapt to disruptions, and build differentiation in the market.

The consequences of inaction are already clear: rising operational costs, supply chain disruptions, and loss of competitive advantage. But for businesses that proactively integrate sustainability, the rewards are significant: cost savings, brand strength, access to emerging markets, and new business models.

Historical perspective: the evolution of sustainability

Sustainability, as a concept, dates back decades, but its role in business has evolved significantly.

▶ 1987 – The Brundtland Report: the United Nations defined sustainability as 'meeting the needs of the present without compromising the ability of future generations to meet their own needs.' This introduced the three key dimensions: environmental, economic, and social sustainability [164].

▶ 1998 – The Triple Bottom Line (TBL): John Elkington expanded on this idea, arguing that businesses should measure success not only by profit but also by their social and environmental impact. This marked a shift toward holistic corporate responsibility [165].

▶ 2000s – Rise of ESG Reporting: Environmental, Social, and Governance (ESG) metrics became a key tool for companies to measure and communicate their sustainability efforts. Initially focused on large corporations, ESG reporting now extends to smaller businesses through supply chain requirements and investor expectations.

▶ 2015 – UN Sustainable Development Goals (SDGs): the 17 global goals provided a blueprint for sustainable progress, reinforcing sustainability as a global priority beyond corporate interests.

While the terms and frameworks have evolved, the core idea remains the same: sustainability is essential for long-term resilience, market relevance, and innovation. Today, companies that fail to integrate sustainability risk falling behind, while those that embrace it gain a strategic advantage.

Is sustainability nothing but a barrier and obstacle to economic growth?

As I finish writing this book, the geopolitical landscape is more turbulent than ever, and more days than not, I find myself feeling anxious about the future. After the 2024 U.S. elections, sustainability is rapidly losing traction, at least in the U.S. Skepticism around ESG initiatives is growing, not just in politics, but also in the technology sector and the broader economy [166].

The impact is already visible. In Q4 2024, corporate earnings calls mentioned ESG fewer times than at any point in the last four years [166]. Meanwhile, investor interest is cooling: funding for ESG-focused technology startups dropped by 54% year-over-year [166]. Once-booming sectors like carbon offset marketplaces and carbon accounting platforms have seen a sharp decline from their 2021 and 2022 peaks [166].

This decline means:

▶ Less focus on ESG: companies are talking about ESG far less than in previous years.

▶ Market shift: investors may be moving away from sustainability initiatives and focusing on short-term financial gains.

▶ Regulatory/political factors: ESG has become politically controversial in some regions, making many companies hesitant to discuss or prioritize sustainability efforts.

The shift is undeniable: where sustainability was once a strategic priority, it is now increasingly seen as a cost, a compliance burden, or even a political liability. But does this mean sustainability is a dead-end for businesses? Far from it.

This growing skepticism around ESG and sustainability initiatives is not new. One of the most persistent arguments against sustainability is that it slows economic growth and burdens businesses with unnecessary regulations. Many companies and policymakers argue that sustainability policies, especially stricter ESG regulations, increase bureaucracy, inflate costs, and divert attention from core business priorities.

But is this perception accurate? Do sustainability regulations truly stifle growth, or do they, in fact, drive long-term innovation, efficiency, and competitiveness?

Sustainability regulations: a barrier or a catalyst for innovation?

The imposition of stricter sustainability regulations has long sparked debate. Critics argue that these policies increase bureaucratic burdens, forcing companies to navigate complex compliance processes that drain time, resources, and investment from core business priorities, including innovation [167].

For smaller firms, the challenge is even greater. Meeting sustainability requirements often demands significant financial investment: from upgrading production processes to implementing reporting systems. Some argue that these costs can divert funds from research and development, stifling creativity and competitiveness [167]. Additionally, rigid compliance standards can lead to short-term operational inefficiencies, further discouraging investment in new technologies.

However, not everyone agrees with this perspective. Proponents of sustainability regulations argue that, rather than stifling innovation, these policies often serve as a catalyst for it. Stricter environmental rules push companies to rethink processes, develop cleaner technologies, and create more efficient business models.

A compelling argument for this view is Porter's Hypothesis, developed by Michael Porter and Claas van der Linde. They suggest that well-designed regulations can spur two types of innovation [168, 169]: Process Innovation and Product Innovation (more about these a bit later).

Porter's Hypothesis suggests that while companies may resist regulations initially, they ultimately benefit from the new efficiencies and market differentiation these policies drive [168, 169].

Several studies reinforce this idea. Rubashkina et al. (2015) found that stricter environmental regulations did not reduce innovation levels, instead prompting industries to adapt and maintain competitive output [170].

Beyond mandatory rules, voluntary sustainability frameworks, such as the Global Reporting Initiative (GRI), the Carbon Disclosure Project (CDP), and the UN Global Compact, play an equally significant role. While not legally binding, they provide market incentives that encourage businesses to integrate sustainability into strategy.

Ultimately, **whether mandatory or voluntary, sustainability regulations,** are not merely compliance requirements, they **are shaping the future of business innovation.** An increasing body of research indicates that well-designed environmental regulations can foster innovation and enhance productivity [171, 172, 173].

Overcoming four barriers to sustainable innovation

Despite increasing global sustainability pressures, many companies resist innovation in this space due to several barriers. Understanding these barriers is essential before exploring how sustainability can actually drive innovation.

Barrier 1: short-term thinking over long-term gains

For decades, businesses measured success primarily by financial performance, with short-term shareholder returns taking precedence. However, the environmental consequences of business activities are now undeniable, and pressure from regulators, consumers, and investors is forcing companies to rethink their priorities.

Despite this shift, many companies still resist sustainability because they view it as an added cost rather than a long-term investment. Although this short-term mindset is gaining traction again, it remains outdated. Firms that integrate sustainability strategically are not just meeting regulatory requirements, they are building resilience, innovation, and market advantages.

Why must companies adapt? There are at least three reasons why companies can no longer afford to stand still:

1. Regulations are tightening: governments worldwide are raising sustainability standards, requiring businesses to integrate social and environmental objectives into their strategies. ESG reporting is now a key performance measure, not just an optional initiative.

2. Consumer expectations are changing: buyers increasingly demand products and services that align with sustainable values from energy efficiency to fair labour practices. Companies that fail to adapt, risk losing market share.

3. Sustainability as a competitive edge: businesses investing in green technology and ethical sourcing are proving more resilient in volatile markets.

The evidence says: sustainability boosts performance. Contrary to the belief that sustainability hurts profitability, research shows it can enhance innovation and efficiency:

▶ Porter's Hypothesis: stricter environmental regulations do not stifle business growth, they push companies to innovate, reducing costs and creating new revenue streams [168].

▶ Kumar Dey et al. (2020) found that sustainable practices improve operational efficiency, foster innovation, and strengthen brand reputation [174]. Addressing issues like labour conditions and community engagement enhances workforce motivation and stakeholder trust [174].

▶ Long-term financial benefits: companies that adopt sustainability-driven strategies don't just mitigate risk, they unlock new market opportunities and achieve stronger long-term financial performance [175, 165, 176].

Sustainability and profitability are not mutually exclusive; rather, they reinforce each other in a virtuous cycle.

Barrier 2: regulatory compliance as a burden, not an opportunity

For many businesses, sustainability regulations are seen as an added burden: a bureaucratic hurdle that requires significant resources, increases operational costs, and limits flexibility. Critics argue that such regulations divert investment from core activities, including innovation, by imposing compliance processes that consume valuable time and resources [167].

Small and medium-sized enterprises (SMEs) are particularly vulnerable to this challenge. Meeting sustainability requirements often demands heavy investments in new technologies and complex reporting frameworks, making compliance disproportionately difficult for smaller firms with limited resources. Additionally, stringent regulations may enforce rigid standards and operational constraints, which some businesses fear could stifle creativity and innovation [167].

However, this perception overlooks a key reality: well-structured sustainability regulations do not stifle innovation, they drive it.

One of the most influential perspectives on how regulation drives innovation comes from economists Michael Porter and Claas van der Linde, known as *Porter's Hypothesis*. Porter's Hypothesis argues that properly designed regulations can stimulate innovation in two main ways [168, 169]:

1. Process innovation: companies improve efficiency and reduce waste by implementing technological advancements within their production lines or through 'end-of-pipe' solutions. For example, Coca-Cola has implemented

innovative water-recycling technologies in its bottling plants, significantly reducing water usage and improving efficiency [168, 169].

2. Product innovation: firms develop less polluting and higher-performing products that align with sustainability goals and consumer demands [168, 169]. Examples include the rise of electric vehicles as an alternative to traditional gasoline-powered cars and FLOKK's glue-free chairs, which are designed for easy disassembly and full recyclability.

Porter's Hypothesis establishes a causal link between environmental regulation, innovation, and improved business performance [168, 169]. Rather than imposing unnecessary costs, regulations force businesses to rethink outdated practices and to create long-term gains.

More research support Porter's Hypothesis that regulations enhance competitiveness. Jaffe and Palmer (1997) also confirmed that well-designed environmental regulations can encourage innovation, improve efficiency, and enhance market competitiveness [177]. A study by Rubashkina et al. (2015) further demonstrates that stricter environmental regulations do not lead to reduced innovation levels. Instead, industries adapt by altering inputs or improving productivity, maintaining their innovative output [170].

Two major regulatory frameworks in Europe; the CSRD and the EU Green Deal, offer real-world examples of how policy can become a catalyst for innovation and long-term transformation. The EU's Corporate Sustainability Reporting Directive (CSRD) which came into effect on 5 January 5, 2023, and which applies not only to companies based in the EU, but also to non-EU companies generating substantial revenue within the EU market, is one of the most significant regulatory frameworks influencing sustainability innovation [178]. Initially perceived as a costly compliance requirement, the CSRD has, in reality, enhanced transparency, accountability, and investor confidence. By requiring companies to disclose environmental and social impacts, the directive pushes organizations to develop more sustainable business models and align operations with long-term market trends.

Similarly, the EU Green Deal has introduced policies aimed at transforming industries to meet climate goals. While some businesses resisted these policies due to short-term cost concerns, they have led to groundbreaking innovations in renewable energy, circular economy models, and sustainable supply chains. Companies that adapted early to these regulations are now seeing competitive advantages over those lagging behind.

Taken together, these examples show that compliance isn't a burden, it's a powerful driver of opportunity.

While businesses may initially resist sustainability regulations, evidence shows that compliance drives efficiency, innovation, and long-term resilience. Companies that embrace sustainability regulations strategically not only ensure compliance but gain a first-mover advantage in evolving markets. Regulatory frameworks do not exist to punish businesses, they exist to push industries toward smarter, more efficient, and more sustainable solutions.

Sustainability regulations are not just compliance obligations, they are catalysts for transformation. Companies that adapt and innovate within this framework will emerge as leaders in the new economy.

Barrier 3: outdated business models that don't fit sustainability

For many businesses, sustainability is treated as an add-on to their existing operations, rather than a fundamental shift in how they create and deliver value. Traditional business models, built around linear consumption (take–make–dispose), often struggle to accommodate sustainability principles such as resource efficiency, circularity, and long-term resilience. Instead of rethinking their operations, many companies attempt to force sustainability into outdated frameworks, leading to inefficiencies and missed opportunities [179].

Traditional business models are becoming outdated, limiting companies' ability to adapt to evolving market demands and sustainability challenges. Several key factors are driving this shift:

▶ Technological disruptions enable smarter business models: the technological revolution is reshaping industries, allowing businesses to operate more efficiently and more sustainably. AI, 3D printing, and virtual conferencing are reducing emissions and enabling smarter production methods [180]. Virtual meetings and conferences cut CO_2 emissions by 94% and total energy consumption by 90% [180].

▶ Consumer preferences are changing rapidly: younger generations, especially Gen Z and Millennials, are shifting toward sustainability-focused consumption [181]. The sharing economy is booming – tools, electric bikes, scooters, and even cars are increasingly shared instead of owned [182]. Statista's Consumer Insights survey (July 2023–June 2024) states that only 54% of Gen Z in the U.S. believe car ownership is important, compared to 69% of Baby Boomers, highlighting the shift away from ownership models [181]. The sharing economy grew from $113 billion in 2021 to nearly $150 billion in 2023 and is projected to reach $800 billion by 2031 [182].

▶ Regulatory pressures are reshaping business expectations: Governments and regulatory bodies are enforcing sustainability requirements that make traditional business models obsolete. The Right to Repair law in the EU requires manufacturers to make repairs affordable and accessible, shifting businesses toward longer product lifecycles [183].

So, how can new business models turn sustainability from a cost into a competitive advantage?

To thrive in a sustainability-driven economy, businesses must rethink their models from the ground up. Rather than viewing sustainability as a cost centre, companies should integrate it into value creation strategies [184]:

▶ Circular economy models: reducing waste and maximizing resource efficiency by designing products for reuse, repair, and recyclability [184].

▶ Subscription and product-as-a-service models: shifting from ownership-based models to leasing, renting, and reuse, extending product lifespans [184].

▶ Zero-waste manufacturing: implementation of closed-loop systems to minimize waste generation [184].

Here are several real-life examples that lead to these changes:

▶ Ikea's buy-back and repair programs: in response to growing regulations and consumer demand for sustainability, IKEA now offers buy-back programs for used furniture [185]. This initiative extends product lifecycles, reduces landfill waste, and aligns with circular economy principles.

▶ FLOKK's modular, glue-free furniture: FLOKK designs office chairs with modular components that allow for easy repairs, recycling, and disassembly. This sustainable furniture reduces production waste and ensures that materials can be reused rather than discarded.

▶ The rise of the sharing economy: businesses like Hyre, Lime Micromobility, Rent the Runway or in Norway Bysykkel, Voi are capitalizing on consumer demand for access over ownership. This trend reduces overproduction, minimizes waste, and maximizes resource efficiency.

Companies that fail to adapt their business models to sustainability trends risk becoming obsolete. Regulatory pressures, shifting consumer expectations, and rapid technological advancements require businesses to embrace circularity, efficiency, and innovation.

As Jørgensen and Pedersen outline in their RESTART framework, businesses must [184]:

▶ Take responsibility for their negative externalities.

▶ Provide solutions that mitigate or neutralize environmental and social harm.

▶ Shift from product-centric to service-based logic.

The message is clear: the future belongs to businesses that embed sustainability into their core strategies, not those that try to retrofit outdated models.

Barrier 4: perceived high costs of sustainability innovation

A common concern among businesses is that sustainability initiatives are too expensive, requiring large upfront investments that may not yield immediate financial returns. Critics argue that sustainable innovation diverts resources away from core business activities and requires costly overhauls of existing processes [167].

Many companies, especially SMEs, hesitate to embrace sustainable innovation due to fears of higher operational costs, compliance expenses, and uncertainty about long-term benefits. However, research and real-world examples show that these fears are often misguided.

Contrary to the belief that sustainability is merely a financial burden, research demonstrates that it actually enhances business performance through cost savings, efficiency improvements, and competitive advantages [168, 169].

▶ Energy efficiency reduces costs: companies that invest in energy-efficient technologies and resource optimization see significant reductions in operational expenses [186]. For example, businesses that switch to renewable energy sources and smart-grid technology report lower electricity bills and improved energy resilience [187].

▶ Circular economy models minimize waste: firms embracing circular economy principles, such as recycling, refurbishing, and reusing materials, can drastically cut costs by reducing raw material dependency and waste disposal expenses [186, 188].

▶ Process innovation enhances profitability: companies implementing sustainable process innovations, such as water recycling systems, lean manufacturing, and carbon tracking, benefit from improved efficiency, lower waste, and regulatory compliance advantages [188, 187].

Studies confirm that sustainability-driven organizations achieve better financial and operational outcomes:

▶ Masocha (2018) found a positive correlation between environmental sustainability, innovation, and cost reductions [175].

▶ Zhou et al. (2023) demonstrated that firms with strong ESG performance are more likely to develop cost-saving innovations in green technologies, governance mechanisms, and social practices [165].

▶ Kumar Dey et al. (2020) highlighted that sustainable practices improve efficiency, foster brand loyalty, and strengthen investor confidence [174].

Sustainability should not be seen as an expense; it is an investment in future resilience, cost efficiency, and market leadership. Companies that integrate energy efficiency, circular business models, and process innovations not only reduce long-term costs, but also gain a competitive edge in the evolving market landscape. The businesses that adapt now will be the ones that thrive in a sustainability-driven economy.

Now that we've explored why companies struggle, let's shift our focus to how sustainability is becoming an engine for innovation.

Case study: BIR AS – pioneering sustainable innovation in waste management

Sustainability is no longer an option; it is a business necessity. Yet, many companies struggle to integrate sustainability with innovation due to regulatory uncertainty, financial risks, and resistance to change. BIR AS, one of Norway's largest waste management companies, offers a compelling example of how organizations can navigate these barriers while driving sustainable transformation. Through technological advancements, strategic partnerships, and a focus on fostering a strong innovation culture, BIR demonstrates how sustainability can become a catalyst for long-term success rather than a compliance burden.

About BIR AS

BIR AS is responsible for waste management services for over 386,100 residents across ten municipalities in Norway. Founded in 2002 but with historical roots dating back to 1881, BIR has evolved into a leader in environmental responsibility, offering waste solutions, consulting, and services to businesses and industries. In 2023, the company formalized its sustainability strategy, focusing on four key areas: environmental and climate responsibility, resource valorization, responsible management and operations, and the development of people and culture [189].

BIR is not just responding to regulatory pressure; it is actively shaping the future of waste management through innovation. One of its most ambitious projects is the planned carbon capture facility at Rådalen, which aims to capture 100,000 tons of CO_2 annually, significantly reducing fossil emissions from waste incineration [189]. However, as CEO Atle Tvedt Pedersen explains, **making sustainability investments work in practice requires more than just ambition** [190].

Overcoming barriers to sustainable innovation

When asked about the biggest obstacles companies face in sustainable innovation, he highlighted several challenges [190].

First, regulatory and political uncertainty often makes long-term investment planning difficult due to frequent changes in taxes, regulations, and market conditions. Cost concerns are also significant. Sustainability projects typically require substantial upfront investments with uncertain financial returns. For instance, BIR's carbon capture facility requires more than NOK 1 billion, and the project is contingent on funding from national sources such as Enova or CLIMT programs. Without that support, the entire initiative could stall [190].

Second, market dynamics further complicate things. Waste is treated as a commodity that moves across borders, influenced by global competition. Local companies must navigate unique Norwegian taxes, such as the incineration tax, as well as stricter national emission requirements, factors that make it harder to maintain competitive pricing while investing in sustainability [190].

Third, on top of these external pressures, internal cultural barriers also play a role. Companies often struggle with resistance to new ideas, particularly if they lack a strong innovation culture that embraces learning, experimentation, and psychological safety [190].

Despite these barriers, Atle argues that companies must view sustainability as an enabler of innovation rather than a cost centre. 'If it is sustainable, it must also be economically sustainable,' he explains, underscoring the need for business models that align environmental responsibility with financial viability [190].

The role of innovation culture

Beyond large-scale infrastructure projects, BIR recognizes that true innovation starts with people. The company has invested heavily in developing an innovation culture where employees feel psychologically safe to propose ideas, experiment, and collaborate [190].

One important initiative is BIR's psychological safety program, which encourages open feedback and collaborative decision-making. Starting with top management, the program is being gradually rolled out to lower levels of the hierarchy. Efforts have focused on improving the meeting culture, encourage vulnerability in leadership, and create a workplace where employees feel confident voicing new ideas. Particular attention is paid to identifying when someone does not feel safe, helping them lower their 'guards' and be brave enough to ask for help. The goal is to ensure that when someone speaks up, they know it will not be used against them [190].

In parallel, BIR actively collaborates with universities such as UiB, SINTEF, and NORCE, as well as startups, to bring fresh perspectives into waste management innovation. By fostering a culture where learning and external input are valued, the company ensures continuous adaptation [190].

Project prioritization is also a critical element. Atle highlights the importance of knowing when to kill projects that are not viable. 'Many innovations die due to a lack of transfer from R&D to commercialization. Killing bad ideas early is just as important as nurturing good ones,' he notes [190].

Managing expectations and response times is equally crucial. Atle also acknowledges that waiting for decisions or responses on project proposals can be highly demotivating for employees: 'If you put in a lot of effort and don't get feedback, it's discouraging.' This can also influence innovation culture and psychological safety. 'Prioritization means some projects move forward while others are put on hold, and that can be tough,' he explains. Ensuring clear communication and structured follow-ups is crucial for maintaining psychological safety and motivation within teams [190].

Lessons for forward-thinking leaders

BIR's approach offers valuable lessons for leaders across industries who are looking to drive sustainable innovation:

- ▶ Everything starts from the top! It has to be strongly anchored at the top management.

- ▶ Long-term commitment is essential. Sustainable innovation requires persistence, particularly when external conditions (e.g., regulations, funding availability) are unpredictable.

- ▶ Financial sustainability must align with environmental goals. If sustainability initiatives cannot be economically justified, they risk being abandoned when budgets tighten.

- ▶ Psychological safety fuels innovation. Employees must feel safe to experiment, fail, and propose unconventional ideas.

- ▶ Collaboration accelerates impact. Working with universities, startups, and policymakers can help bridge knowledge gaps and de-risk innovation efforts.

- ▶ Know when to pivot or stop. Not all ideas will succeed, and leaders must develop discipline to cut losses when necessary.

- ▶ Clear feedback and decision-making processes matter. Delayed responses or uncertainty about priorities can hinder engagement and innovation. Leaders must create transparency around which projects move forward and why.

BIR AS exemplifies how sustainability and innovation can reinforce each other when approached strategically. By investing in both cutting-edge technology and cultural transformation, the company is not just meeting environmental targets; it is shaping the future of waste management. For leaders looking to embed sustainability into their business models, BIR's journey offers a roadmap for overcoming obstacles and unlocking new opportunities.[2]

Sustainability as a driver for innovation

Sustainability is no longer just a compliance requirement – it is a catalyst for innovation. Companies that proactively integrate sustainability into their business models develop new capabilities, unlock market opportunities, and enhance resilience in a rapidly evolving landscape. Sustainability-driven innovation is reshaping industries, influencing everything from product design and manufacturing to supply chain operations and business models.

However, the loudest forces driving innovation through sustainability are the market and regulator changes. As seen in Porter's Hypothesis, regulatory demands do not hinder innovation; they stimulate it by creating a level playing field and pushing industries to develop cutting-edge solutions. At the same time, consumer expectations are rapidly shifting, demanding that businesses take sustainability seriously.

Market-driven sustainability trends

While regulations play a crucial role in driving sustainability-driven innovation, **the strongest force pushing businesses toward change is the market itself**. Consumers, investors, and industry stakeholders are demanding greater transparency, responsibility, and sustainable practices, forcing companies to innovate or risk becoming irrelevant.

Businesses that fail to adapt are facing declining customer trust, reduced investment opportunities, and increasing competitive pressures. Meanwhile, those that embrace sustainability are gaining market share, investor confidence, and long-term profitability.

---

[2] This case study was developed independently. I have no financial ties to BIR AS, nor was I compensated for including them in this book.

The following trends illustrate how market forces are shaping the sustainability agenda and accelerating innovation.

▸ Growing consumer demand for sustainable products: a 71% increase in online searches for sustainable products between 2016–2021 demonstrates a clear shift in purchasing behaviour [191]. A total of 75% of millennials factor sustainability into their purchasing decisions [192]. Accenture research highlights that over half of consumers are willing to pay a premium for products designed for reuse or recycling [193]. These trends underscore a shift toward brands that prioritize environmental sustainability, aligning with consumer values and expectations.

▸ Regulations driving business innovation: the EU's Right to Repair law is forcing manufacturers to develop products that are repairable, durable, and modular, reshaping industries and disrupting the traditional buy-use-dispose model [183]. Legislative measures to combat CO_2 emissions are driving new innovations, such as the Northern Lights project on Carbon Capture and Storage (CCS) in Norway and Hydrogen production initiatives.

▸ Investor prioritization of ESG metrics: companies with strong ESG ratings attract more investment, reduce financial risks, and future-proof their operations. A study by Kroll, analyzing 13,000 companies, found that firms with higher ESG ratings outperformed their lower-rated peers, with ESG leaders achieving an average annual return of 12.9% compared to 8.6% for laggards [194].

These insights highlight the imperative for businesses to intensify their commitment to sustainability. Companies that embrace sustainability not only drive innovation but also secure long-term competitive advantages.

Consumer awareness of the environmental and health impacts of chemicals and plastics has risen sharply. **Today's consumers are not just passive buyers, they are active decision-makers**

who demand transparency, ethical sourcing, and sustainable alternatives. They are increasingly willing to switch brands based on ethical considerations, a trend accelerated by social media and rapid information sharing.

Sustainability and trust: a competitive advantage

Trust is emerging as a critical driver of consumer behaviour and business success. Research by Reichheld et al. (2023) emphasizes that sustainability plays a central role in building trust, particularly among younger generations [195]. As purchasing power shifts to millennials and Gen Z, businesses have a unique opportunity to cultivate long-term loyalty by embedding sustainability into their core offerings.

This demographic shift presents a strategic priority; organizations that fail to align with these values risk losing relevance [195], while those that embrace sustainability will shape the future of business and innovation.

Conclusion: turning sustainability into strategic action

Sustainability is no longer an optional initiative, it is a strategic driver of innovation, resilience, and competitive advantage. Businesses that integrate sustainability future-proof themselves against risks, attract investment, and meet evolving consumer expectations.

Key takeaways from this chapter

▶ Sustainability is no longer optional, it's a strategic lever for innovation, resilience, and long-term business growth.

▶ Companies that proactively integrate sustainability outperform those that treat it as a compliance exercise or cost centre.

▶ Regulatory frameworks and consumer expectations are accelerating sustainable innovation where early movers gain competitive advantage.

▶ Embedding sustainability into business models, product design, and supply chains opens new market opportunities and drives operational efficiency.

▶ Effective leadership means aligning teams, rethinking outdated models, and treating sustainability as a core strategy, not an afterthought.

For you as a leader, the challenge is not just understanding sustainability's importance but implementing it effectively.

Five actionable steps that you can start taking today

1. Start thinking of sustainability and innovation as one strategy
Sustainability should be a core business function, not an afterthought. To stay competitive, make it an essential part of your strategic thinking.

2. Rethink product development and business models
Start evaluating whether your products and business models can be circular, energy-efficient, or resource-optimized. Brainstorm new approaches: can your company shift from ownership to service-based models, such as leasing, subscriptions, or buy-back programs?

Assess your supply chain and production methods: Are there opportunities to reduce waste, increase efficiency, or incorporate renewable resources? Explore circularity.

3. Explore shifts in consumer mindset and reevaluate your market
Reassess your core customer base: how have your customers' values, expectations, and purchasing behaviours shifted?

Identify new market segments: are there underserved or emerging groups that prioritize sustainability and innovation?

Explore new ways to engage consumers: can your company offer sustainable alternatives, transparent supply chains, or new service models that align with evolving demands?

Consider new customer segments that value sustainability: consumers and investors increasingly demand sustainable business practices. Studies show that 75% of millennials consider sustainability in their purchasing decisions, and ESG-focused companies attract stronger investment returns. Meeting these expectations builds trust, enhances brand loyalty, and strengthens financial resilience.

4. Assess your team's readiness for sustainability

Map out where your team stands: who are the innovators and early adopters? Identify employees who are already advocating sustainability; they will be your key drivers of change.

By identifying internal sustainability leaders, you can leverage their influence to build momentum across the organization.

5. Identify your allies in driving transformation

You need strategic allies at the managerial level and above to build alignment and secure long-term commitment.

Brainstorm: map for yourself who are the decision-makers that can champion sustainability. Which departments or leaders are already engaged?

Map out who can support your sustainability initiatives, whether through funding, strategic alignment, or operational execution. The stronger your network of allies, the greater the chance of success in embedding sustainability into your company's DNA.

***

For additional tools related to this chapter, visit: vinco.no/future-fit-innovation-resources

Chapter 8
Will innovation thrive or stagnate?

Innovation is not a magic formula – it's a commitment

Innovation does not happen just because you adopt a framework. It will not emerge simply because you appoint a Head of Innovation. Nor will it suddenly appear because you have creative individuals or a diverse team.

Innovation is a process shaped by many factors: people, culture, leadership, and external influences. It happens in a complex and dynamic environment where individuals act and drive change. Organizations, like living systems, are influenced by both internal and external forces, and so is innovation. There is no shortcut, no magic formula that will transform your company into an innovative powerhouse overnight. It takes time, effort, and a deep commitment to continuous learning, experimentation, and adaptation.

They say that becoming an expert in any field requires at least 10,000 hours of practice; roughly ten years of dedication. So why do we assume innovation is any different? Why do we believe that implementing a single framework will suddenly make an organization innovative when experience tells us that mastery takes time? You and I both know that sustaining innovation is not built in a day.

This final chapter will help you reflect on:

▶ The critical insights from across the book: how individual beliefs, team dynamics, organizational structures, and contextual factors either block or enable innovation.

▶ Why context matters: how company size, proximity to technology, and even crisis conditions influence how innovation plays out.

▶ The four essential pillars of innovation readiness and how you can assess and strengthen them in your organization.

▶ A practical self-assessment tool to help you reflect on your innovation leadership and culture: the Vindi© Innovation Indicator.

By the end of this chapter, you'll have a clearer understanding of what it really takes to make innovation thrive and how to take your first steps in making it a sustainable part of your organization's DNA.

Overcoming barriers to innovation

In this book, I have highlighted key barriers that often hold companies back from succeeding in innovation.

Moving past the fear of creativity

One of the biggest barriers is creativity, or rather, the discomfort we feel about being creative. Many of us instinctively resist when asked to 'be creative' or 'think outside the box.' We feel pressure, anxiety, or even self-doubt. But the barriers to creativity are not just in our mindset. They also stem from company culture, habits, and established ways of working. Creativity thrives in environments where curiosity is encouraged, openness is nurtured, and new experiences are embraced. If you have team members who hesitate when asked to 'be creative', know that this is normal. Now, you also understand why and what you can do to help them move past it. But remember, truly innovative teams are not those with the most ideas; they are the ones that turn ideas into reality with purpose and strategy.

Functional fixedness: a core barrier to innovation

As I reflect on everything covered in this book, one theme stands out as the single greatest barrier to innovation: fixedness. Functional fixedness is the tendency to see things only as they are, rather than what they could become. It limits our ability to find new solutions and innovate. As we grow older, we all develop functional fixedness, it's an evolutionary advantage that helps us navigate the world efficiently.

Fixedness appears in many forms:

▶ The mindset which thinks 'I am not creative'.

▶ Homogeneous teams that reinforce old ways of thinking.

▶ Fear of the unknown, whether it's new technology or new business models.

▶ Holding to outdated priorities, such as focusing on profit alone while ignoring societal and environmental sustainability.

But the world is changing. Customers are demanding innovation. Employees are demanding better leadership. And as my chemistry teacher liked to say: 'The only constant is change'.

We humans do not resist change itself, we resist uncertainty. But embracing change is what has allowed us to evolve, progress, and thrive.

When it comes to creativity and innovation, however, fixedness doesn't disappear on its own. We must work actively, and sometimes uncomfortably, to challenge what we take for granted.

To break through, we need deliberate techniques that help us look at problems differently. One such method is the Generic Parts Technique. It involves deconstructing an idea, product, or process into its core components and reimagining what each part could become. A technique also used by Apple. Deliberately or not, we will maybe never know. But it worked.

Alternative thinking doesn't just happen, it needs space, encouragement, and permission. As leaders, your job is to make that space real.

The key is to challenge these habits and intentionally create space for alternative thinking.

Embracing diversity: a strength, not a challenge

Breaking free from fixedness also means embracing diversity. While diversity is often discussed as a corporate priority, we still see major gaps. Even in industries that claim to value inclusion, people with disabilities remain overlooked, women, especially women of colour, are underrepresented in leadership, and **homogeneous teams continue to make decisions that impact a diverse world**.

Some argue that diversity creates friction and miscommunication, and research confirms this. But studies also show that this friction is only a challenge if diversity is not managed properly. As a leader, it is your responsibility to create an environment where diverse teams thrive. And the most effective way to do that is by building psychological safety.

Psychological safety: the oxygen of innovation

Psychological safety is not about being nice or avoiding conflict. It is about creating a climate where people feel safe to speak up, challenge ideas, and take risks. It is the confidence that voicing an idea will not lead to embarrassment, punishment, or exclusion.

Innovation cannot survive without debate, collaboration, and experimentation and these only happen when people trust that their input is valued.

Psychological safety is not an organizational policy, it is a property of a group, not the organization as a whole! It is shaped by the leader, by how you respond when someone challenges the status quo. Do you encourage new thinking, or do you shut it down? The way you react determines whether innovation will flourish or fade away.

The role of leadership in a tech-driven world

Leadership is not just about managing tasks and goals. It is about navigating uncertainty, leading people, and responding to external disruptions. One of the fastest-moving forces today is technology.

Technological advancements are evolving at an exponential pace, but their success depends on people's willingness to adopt them. Humans are creatures of habit, resistant to breaking familiar routines. Many fear that technology will take over their jobs, or that they will lose control. We have seen these fears for decades, and yet, the human factor remains more critical than ever.

Technology is not just an efficiency tool, it is a driver of new business models, services, and entire industries. It can also be a force for sustainability. Blockchain enables better resource tracking, 3D printing reduces production waste, and CO_2 capture technologies are reshaping industrial emissions.

Sustainability: an opportunity, not a burden

The environmental impact of human activity is a pressing issue, and businesses must be part of the solution. The outdated mindset of prioritizing profit above all else is fading globally, despite some nations still holding on to short-term profit-focused strategies. This stands in contrast to growing pressure from regulators, consumers, and younger generations demanding sustainable action.

Many argue that sustainability regulations are a burden, but research shows the opposite. Porter's Hypothesis demonstrates that well-designed regulations stimulate process and product innovation. Moreover, whether sustainability efforts are mandatory or voluntary, studies confirm that they drive innovation and enhance productivity. In other words, sustainability is not a barrier to innovation, it is an accelerator.

Innovation in different contexts

Innovation emerges through context, not isolation. **How a company innovates is influenced by its size, its proximity to technological advancements, and its ability to navigate crises.** These factors shape the speed, scope, and impact of innovative efforts. Understanding these contextual differences is key to developing a strategy that works for your organization.

Big vs. small organizations: different strengths, different challenges

Does company size matter for innovation? Research shows that it does. Whether your company is large or small will influence your innovative output, strategy, and barriers to success.

Large organizations are like massive tankers navigating the ocean. They have structured hierarchies, bureaucracies, and decision-making layers that slow them down. Rolling out an innovation from the top to the bottom takes time. The message can be misunderstood, engagement may be lost, and agility is sacrificed. Sudden shifts are nearly impossible; turning the organization requires patience, effort, and long-term commitment.

Small organizations, on the other hand, are like sailing boats: agile, fast, and able to pivot quickly. They can adopt innovations more rapidly because they have fewer hierarchical barriers. Communication is direct, and decisions are executed immediately, minimizing the risk of misalignment. This flexibility enables small firms to adapt faster to market changes [196] and take bigger innovation risks.

However, small firms face a major disadvantage: limited financial and human resources. While they may be more adaptable, their ability to sustain innovation efforts, especially radical ones, is constrained by budgetary and operational limitations. This often becomes a major barrier to scaling new ideas [196, 197, 198, 199].

Big organizations, in contrast, have financial power and resource depth. This allows them to withstand crises better, fund long-term R&D, and take calculated risks [200]. However, their bureaucratic structures often suppress innovation by making it difficult to challenge existing processes.

Company size also influences the type of innovation produced:

▶ Large firms tend to focus on incremental innovation. Since they invest heavily in R&D, they focus on optimizing existing products and processes to maximize efficiency. However, this rationalized approach often limits their ability to pursue radical innovation [201, 202].

▶ Small firms, by contrast, are more likely to pursue radical innovations. Since they lack the resources to compete with established players through efficiency, they use breakthrough innovation as a strategy to disrupt markets and gain a foothold [201, 202].

Proximity to technological advancements

Where a company is located, both geographically and technologically, also shapes its innovative potential.

Firms closer to innovation hubs and cutting-edge research are more likely to generate new knowledge and develop original technologies [203, 204]. These companies benefit from collaboration, knowledge exchange, and resource sharing, all of which accelerate innovation. Being near the technological frontier encourages a more proactive, innovation-driven strategy [203].

For your company, this means:

▶ Following industry trends and staying informed about emerging technologies.

▶ Actively connecting with knowledge hubs: R&D centres, universities, and industry networks.

▶ Engaging in open innovation: collaborating with partners to co-develop solutions.

Companies further from the technological frontier, in contrast, focus more on adoption than creation. Instead of developing 'new-to-the-market' innovations,[3] they prioritize integrating existing technologies into their business models. While this can still drive competitive advantage, it is fundamentally different from pushing the boundaries of technological progress.

If your company wants to leverage technological advancements, it must actively build skilled talent, invest in R&D, and cultivate an innovation mindset [205]. Without these foundations, being physically close to innovation hubs alone will not be enough.

Innovation in times of crisis: a myth or reality?

When COVID-19 hit, a friend of mine proudly proclaimed: 'So good that the crisis hit – finally, we will be innovative!'

At first, this idea puzzled me. I had spent years working with companies on innovation and knew first-hand how difficult it is even in stable times. Why would innovation suddenly thrive in crisis when companies are under immense pressure?

When a crisis hits, the immediate reaction is rarely one of bold creativity. Instead, fear, anxiety, and paralysis take over. Individuals and entire organizations stop to reflect. Businesses cut expenses, freeze projects, and shift to survival mode. Strategies are

---

[3] 'New-to-the-market' innovation is explained on page 193.

reevaluated, and actions become more cautious. So how does that lead to more innovation, or does it lead to it at all?

Does crisis actually boost innovation, or is that just a myth?

The COVID-19 pandemic, the 2008 financial crisis, and the ongoing geopolitical instability of 2024/25 have disrupted economies worldwide. These crises have reshaped markets, changed customer behaviour, and forced companies to adapt. Limitations can be a source of innovation, but not all crises are creative disruptions.

The economist Joseph Schumpeter introduced the concept of creative destruction: the idea that equilibrium must be broken for innovation to emerge. But **breaking equilibrium isn't necessarily synonymous with crisis**. It can simply mean challenging the status quo, intentionally and constructively, and this can be achieved without chaos or collapse.

Crises like financial collapses or geopolitical turmoil, and wars create negative uncertainty leading to paralysis rather than progress.

What the research says?

An OECD study from 2012 measured impacts of the 2008 financial crisis on innovation [200]. The study rejects the assumption that the downturn ignites innovation [200]:

- ▶ New business creation declined. Only a few countries managed to return to pre-crisis levels.

- ▶ Venture capital funding dropped. Investors became risk-averse, leading to fewer breakthrough projects.

- ▶ Patent activity slowed down. Trends in PCT filings showed a significant decline.

The OECD study (2012) identifies several causes to this, which are also common with the COVID-19 crisis: reduced demand on goods and services, reduced liquidity in the financial sector, and limited public budgets [200].

So, does this mean innovation always declines in a crisis? Not necessarily. The research also found that some companies, and countries, known as persistent innovators, not only survive crises but strengthen their innovation capabilities [200].

How to innovate during a crisis?

What separates persistent innovators from companies that struggle? Research highlights three key factors [206, 207]:

1. A strong national innovation system: countries with robust financial institutions, skilled labour, and effective innovation policies weather crises better [207]. While you cannot control this as a company, you can choose to operate in ecosystems that support innovation.

2. Continuous investment in technological capabilities: companies that keep developing technology, even when resources are tight, are better positioned for long-term success [206]. Proximity to innovation hubs plays a major role here, the study confirmed again.

3. A focus on 'new-to-the-market' innovations: companies that introduce truly novel products and services, rather than just incremental improvements, tend to maintain momentum and emerge stronger from crises [206].

'New-to-the-market' innovation: the key to crisis resilience

First iPhone: 'new-to-the-market' innovation

What exactly are 'new-to-the-market' innovations? The Innovation Ambition Matrix (Nagji and Tuff) provides a useful framework [208]:

▷ The core: where you optimize your existing products.

▷ Adjacent: expanding from your existing business into new areas that are related but still unfamiliar to your company.

▶ Transformational: where, according to the Naji and Tuff, you develop breakthroughs and invent things for markets that don't yet exist.

This transformational innovation represents true 'new-to-the-market' products and services; solutions that did not exist before, but the market quickly embraces them as they emerge. The best example is the launch of the iPhone or iPad. These products revolutionized industries, created entirely new categories, and reshaped consumer behaviour. To fully understand what makes an innovation truly 'new-to-the-market', it's helpful to contrast it with the two other categories in the Innovation Ambition Matrix: adjacent and core innovations.

Samsung Galaxy: an adjacent 'new-to-the-company' innovation

When Samsung later introduced its phone: the Samsung Galaxy, it was not a new-to-the-market innovation but rather an adjacent innovation: 'new-to-the-company' innovation, but not new to the market. Similarly, in Norway, a company had a huge success with home delivery of pet food. Innovation Norway recognized them as highly innovative and awarded them public funding. While their business model was efficient and profitable, pet food delivery itself was not a new-to-the-market innovation, it had been done before in other countries.

New versions of iPhones and Samsung Galaxy: incremental innovation

Finally, incremental innovation, or what Nagji and Tuff call core innovation, involves making small improvements to existing products or services. For example, each new version of the iPhone or Samsung Galaxy falls into this category. While these updates may introduce better cameras, processors, or design tweaks, they do not fundamentally change the market the way the first iPhone did.

Conclusion: innovation requires more than good intentions

Companies often make ambitious innovation goals, send employees to training programs, and discuss transformation strategies. Then in reality they do not have the time, effort, or resources to do it and many fail to follow through.

Innovation is not a five-day workshop. It is not a 'quick fix' formula. It's about embedding a culture of innovation at all levels.

✓ Individuals make teams.

✓ Teams create organizations.

✓ Organizations operate within a broader context.

Many organizations fail because they focus too much on rigid frameworks while neglecting people. Innovation happens through people, and without an empowering environment, no methodology will work.

Short-term thinking is the enemy of innovation. Most companies prioritize immediate results, but breakthrough innovation culture takes time. Investors and owners want quick wins, but the most transformative innovations often take years to materialize.

Innovation is uncertain by nature. It is the promise that today's idea may become tomorrow's game-changing product or service. But because this future is unclear, many companies hesitate to invest in it. Overcoming this hesitation is what separates truly innovative organizations from the rest.

This context: company size, technological proximity, and crisis preparedness, determines also whether innovation will thrive or stagnate. Understanding and adapting to these factors is what sets truly innovative organizations apart from those that struggle to change.

Effective implantation of innovation requires (model adapted from [209]):

▶ Innovation processes: structured systems to guide innovation from idea generation to execution.

▶ Frameworks and techniques: methodologies such as design thinking, minimum viable product (MVP), open innovation strategies, and jobs to be done, etc.

▶ Knowledge and experience: a strong foundation in innovation management, enabling organizations to evaluate risks, assess market potential, and build innovation capacity through learning, knowledge transfer, and strategic partnerships.

▶ An innovation culture: the most critical yet often missing element that determines whether innovation succeeds or fails.

Most companies focus on and have in place the first three elements. However, even with robust processes, proven frameworks, and knowledge transfer, innovation will stall in an organization where innovation culture is not embedded. If employees fear failure, if leadership does not actively support new ideas, or if risk-taking is discouraged, innovation efforts will collapse. Building an innovation culture means fostering psychological safety, rewarding experimentation, and embedding innovation into the company's DNA – ensuring that innovation is not a one-time initiative but a continuous, evolving process.

This book goes beyond typical innovation processes and a widely used frameworks – it **addresses the missing piece that many companies struggle with building an innovation culture.** This is where the book **fills the gap.** It provides you, the leader, with the foundational understanding necessary to navigate human behaviours, the behaviours of individuals who make up teams and ultimately shape organizational dynamics.

You are now equipped to recognize how your leadership influences situations, how team dynamics evolve, and how context impacts both individual and organizational innovation.

To be truly innovative, organizations must assess where they stand on all four pillars and take deliberate steps to strengthen any weaknesses. A company that successfully balances structured processes, effective frameworks, expertise, and culture will not only generate new ideas but also transform them into meaningful, long-lasting innovations.

Key takeaways from this chapter

▶ Innovation is not a quick fix or a one-off initiative, it requires long-term commitment, leadership support, and a strong cultural foundation.

▶ The biggest barrier to innovation is fixedness – in mindset, behaviour, processes, and strategy. Overcoming it is essential for creativity and adaptability.

▶ Sustaining innovation depends on more than frameworks and tools: it needs empowered people, psychological safety, and inclusive leadership.

▶ Innovation thrives in context: factors like company size, crisis readiness, technological proximity, and cultural flexibility all influence your success.

▶ The four pillars of innovation readiness – processes, frameworks, knowledge, and culture – must work together. Culture is often the missing piece.

▶ Tools like the Vindi© Innovation Indicator help assess and strengthen the human side of innovation because leadership behaviour and team dynamics are what make or break innovation efforts.

Assessing your innovation readiness with Vindi© Innovation Indicator

Understanding the four key pillars – innovation processes, frameworks, knowledge, and culture – is critical. However, many companies overestimate their innovation maturity. They may have frameworks like design thinking, lean startup, and MVP, but they lack the right culture and behaviours to make innovation sustainable.

This is where Vindi© Innovation Indicator comes in.

Vindi© is an Innovation Indicator that helps organizations assess their innovation culture and behaviours. Unlike typical innovation assessments that focus on strategies and processes, Vindi© evaluates the human side of innovation: the attitudes, leadership behaviours, and organizational dynamics that enable (or block) innovation.

Why is Vindi© valuable?

Vindi measures five key behaviours essential for fostering innovation:

1. Networking and diversity: how well do employees engage with different perspectives?

2. Experimentation: is the company comfortable with trying new things and learning from failures?

3. Questioning: do employees and leaders challenge the status quo?

4. Observing: are insights from past experiences used to improve innovation?

5. Leadership support: how does top management influence the innovation culture?

Try Vindi© for free

As a reader of this book, you have the opportunity to **try Vindi©ₒ for free** and receive a simplified but **personalized assessment** of your innovation behaviour. While a full organizational analysis requires input from multiple team members, this individual assessment will help you:

▶ Reflect on your own innovation behaviours: how you approach networking, experimentation, questioning, and observing.

▶ Understand how your leadership style influences innovation: are you or your management fostering an environment where new ideas thrive?

▶ Identify areas for personal growth to become a stronger innovation leader.

Take the next step – assess your innovation approach today. Try Vindi© for free at vinco.no/vinco-vindi and start strengthening your leadership's impact on innovation.

A call to action

Throughout this book, we've looked at innovation from many angles: individual mindset, team dynamics, and organizational strategy. The cases of BIR and Sparebanken Norge bring these elements together in practice. Both organizations demonstrate that innovation is not driven by isolated tools or a single heroic individual, but by cultures that support learning, openness, and long-term thinking.

BIR showed how investing in psychological safety and structured prioritization can drive sustainability-led innovation. Sparebanken Norge demonstrated how technology and tradition can be aligned through cross-functional collaboration and shared values, while also providing a clear example of high psychological safety in action.

These cases prove that when strategy, culture, and people are integrated, innovation doesn't just survive, it thrives. They are powerful examples of innovation implemented right.

As you step forward, remember that transformation starts with a single decision: to think, act, and lead differently.

As Siren Sundland said to me in our interview: 'We don't always get it right – but we get it often' [163].

Before closing this book, I encourage you to take a moment and reflect.

- ▶ What's the first step you will take to drive innovation in your team or company?

- ▶ What will you change about your approach to leadership, creativity, or organizational culture?

- ▶ Write down three concrete actions that you will put into action.

What three things from this book can you start implementing today?

1.

2.

3.

The question is not whether innovation is possible in your organization, but whether you are willing to create the conditions for it to thrive.

The best innovators don't just learn – they act.

Now, it's your turn.

***

Thank you for reading my book. I hope it sparked new thinking, and even more importantly, action.

Ready to take the next step?

I've created additional tools, checklists, and resources to help you apply these ideas in your own context. Visit: **vinco.no/ future-fit-innovation-resources**

Some materials are exclusive to book readers – follow the instructions on the page to access them.

This is where your journey continues.

About the author

Barbara Salopek is an innovation strategist, founder of Vinco Innovation, and adjunct lecturer at BI Norwegian Business School. With over two decades of experience, she helps organizations turn ideas into real-world impact through innovation strategies, culture-building, and hands-on leadership of transformative projects.

Passionate about making innovation more human and less abstract, she works with leaders and teams to build cultures that are creative, inclusive, and capable of navigating change. Her work combines deep insight with a touch of rebellious energy: encouraging others to question assumptions, embrace diverse perspectives, and take bold steps toward the future.

In addition to consulting, she regularly gives talks and writes on topics such as innovation leadership, psychological safety, and the future of sustainable business. Her thought leadership has been featured in articles, webinars, and industry forums across Europe.

Originally from Croatia, she has lived and worked in four different countries and has called Norway home for the past 20 years.

A multilingual entrepreneur with a global mindset, she believes that resilience, curiosity, and collaboration are at the heart of lasting innovation.

Future-Fit Innovation is her first book – a practical and inspiring guide for leaders ready to shape the future by transforming the way they innovate.

www.linkedin.com/in/barbara-salopek/

https://vinco.no/future-fit-innovation/

www.instagram.com/bsalopek/

https://barbarasalopek.com/

Acknowledgements

A friend once told me, 'Barbara, when you start your own business, you discover who your true friends are.' That couldn't be truer. Neither my company, nor this book would have seen the light of day without the incredible support from my family, friends, colleagues, and professional partners.

I want to thank the person who once said to me, 'Barbara, you need to write a book.' I'm sorry I can't recall your name – but back then, I laughed and waved it off, thinking, 'That's just not my thing.' And yet, here we are. 'Overwhelmed' doesn't even begin to describe the feeling, but I am deeply grateful that this long journey has come to life.

Special thanks to Professor Dr. John Bessant for your thoughtful and generous Foreword. Your words beautifully capture the essence of this book, and I'm incredibly thankful for your support.

To my colleagues at BI Norwegian Business School campus Bergen: thank you for being such a source of inspiration. Your openness, curiosity, and brilliant discussions shaped much of this book.

I'm especially grateful to those who read the full manuscript, chapters, or excerpts and generously shared their feedback. Your thoughtful insights helped shape this book in meaningful ways. To all of you, and to those who supported the book with your endorsements: Dr. Renate Kratochvil, Jason Yeoh, Scott Parson, Aslak Sverdrup, Sivert Smedsvig, Dr. Eric Arne Lofquist, Montserrat F. Telseth, Ratko Mutavdzic, Janusz Moskwa, Kathryn Galambos, Alexandra Fehling, Dr. Nathan Davis, Dr. Stig Berge Matthiesen, and Agnieszka Łyniewska – thank you for your belief in this project and your contributions along the way.

A heartfelt thanks to Dr. Renate Kratochvil – your encouragement and belief in me was a turning point. To Annelise Ly, thank you for the early book conversations that helped shape this idea in its infancy.

To my publisher, the team at Practical Inspiration Publishing, and especially Alison Jones, thank you for your expert guidance, patience, and belief in this book's message. Your support helped shape it into a finished work I'm proud of. I'm also grateful to the wonderful PIP author community I'm a part of and for their support as well.

A heartfelt thank you to the talented and up-and-coming illustrator of the book illustrations, Mara Jeger, for translating complex ideas into clear, engaging visuals that bring this book to life.

I would also like to give a big thank you to Atle Tvedt Pedersen and Siren Sundland for generously sharing your insights during our interview, your perspectives added valuable depth to this book.

Thank you, Kari Amble, for your open heart, ever-present support, and for teaching me not just how to write, but how to be myself. You've made a tremendous impact on me.

To the brilliant women, my dear friends and colleagues, who have walked this path before me: Sonja van Uden, Lisbeth Skogseth, Marianne Grung Farsund, and Irene Kinunda Afriyie. Thank you for your inspiration, wisdom, and the generous advice you shared. You helped light the way.

To my dear friends, collaborators, and professional partners: thank you for always cheering me on and supporting the endeavours that led to this book. Your encouragement, insights, and presence, whether through conversations, messages, or quiet acts of support, meant more than I can express. To my extended circle of support, from Norway to Croatia, the U.S., and beyond, thank you. I am truly grateful.

Thank you also to all my SoMe supporters, you know who you are, and I truly appreciate your encouragement and presence throughout this journey.

To everyone who has been part of the Vinco Innovation team, past and present, thank you for embodying the spirit of sustaining innovation. Your dedication, creativity, and belief in our mission have helped shape the work we do and have inspired many of the ideas in this book. I'm grateful for your contributions and for being part of this journey.

And last, but by no means least, my family. Thank you to my amazing husband and our children for your endless love, patience, and those quiet hugs during the most doubtful moments. Mom, thank you for being such an inspiration. To my dear family: my sister, her two fantastic daughters, my brothers, my stepdad, and my cousin Tea – thank you for always being there with advice, encouragement, and love.

_____

I used limited AI-supported tools during the editing process to identify patterns, reduce repetition, and improve clarity, much like one might use any digital tool or seek feedback from human reviewers to enhance structure and language. Every idea, story, and argument in this book is entirely my own, unless otherwise referenced.

References

[1] 'Innovation and commercialization, 2010: McKinsey Global Survey results | McKinsey'. Accessed: 17 February, 2025. [Online]. Available: www.mckinsey. com/capabilities/strategy-and-corporate-finance/our-insights/innovation-and-commercialization-2010-mckinsey-global-survey-results

[2] Cambridge University Press & Assessment 2024, 'Creativity', Cambridge Dictionary. Accessed: 3 October, 2024. [Online]. Available: https://dictionary. cambridge.org/dictionary/english/creativity

[3] Cambridge University Press & Assessment 2024, 'Invention', Cambridge Dictionary. Accessed: 4 October, 2024. [Online]. Available: https://dictionary. cambridge.org/dictionary/english/invention

[4] Cambridge University Press & Assessment 2024, 'Innovation', Cambridge Dictionary. Accessed: 3 October, 2024. [Online]. Available: https://dictionary. cambridge.org/dictionary/english/innovation

[5] J. Hope, 'A Better Mousetrap', American Heritage. [Online]. Available: www. americanheritage.com/better-mousetrap

[6] Smithsonian, 'Mouse Trap', si.edu. [Online]. Available: www.si.edu/object/ mouse-trap:nmah_322315

[7] R. F. Hurley and G. T. M. Hult, 'Innovation, Market Orientation, and Organizational Learning: An Integration and Empirical Examination', *J. Mark.*, vol. 62, no. 3, pp. 42–54, July, 1998, doi: 10.1177/002224299806200303.

[8] P. F. Nunes and T. Breene, *Jumping the S-Curve – How to Beat the Growth Cycle, Get on Top, and Stay There*. Harvard Business Review Press, 2011.

[9] World Bank and World Bank, *Global Economic Prospects, January 2025*. World Bank, 2025, doi: 10.1596/978-1-4648-2147-9.

[10] Boston Consulting Group, 'Reaching New Heights in Uncertain Times', Boston Consulting Group, 2023.

[11] P. F. Drucker, 'The Discipline of Innovation', in *HBR's 10 must reads*, Harvard Business School Publishing Corporation, 2013.

[12] S. Tweedie, 'How the microwave oven was invented by accident', businessinsider.com. Accessed: 11 October, 2024. [Online]. Available: www. businessinsider.com/how-the-microwave-oven-was-invented-by-accident-2015-4

[13] K. Talke, S. Salomo, and A. Kock, 'Top Management Team Diversity and Strategic Innovation Orientation: The Relationship and Consequences for Innovativeness and Performance', *J. Prod. Innov. Manag.*, vol. 28, no. 6, pp. 819–832, November, 2011, doi: 10.1111/j.1540-5885.2011.00851.x.

[14] G. Castellion and S. K. Markham, 'Perspective: New Product Failure Rates: Influence of *A rgumentum ad P opulum* and Self-Interest', *J. Prod. Innov. Manag.*, vol. 30, no. 5, pp. 976–979, September, 2013, doi: 10.1111/j.1540-5885.2012.01009.x.

[15] C. M. Christensen, S. P. Kaufman, and W. C. Shih, 'Innovation Killers: How Financial Tools Destroy Your Capacity to Do New Things', hbr.org. Accessed: 5 October, 2024. [Online]. Available: https://hbr.org/2008/01/innovation-killers-how-financial-tools-destroy-your-capacity-to-do-new-things

[16] Adobe.de, 'Study Reveals Global Creativity Gap', adobe-newsroom.de. Accessed: 18 September, 2022. [Online]. Available: www.adobe-newsroom.de/2012/04/24/study-reveals-global-creativity-gap/

[17] Adobe, 'Creativity Drives Business Success – Key Takeaways From the 2016 State of Create Report', Adobe Blog. Accessed: 18 September, 2022. [Online]. Available: https://blog.adobe.com/en/publish/2016/11/01/2016-state-of-create-report

[18] G. T. Ainsworth-Land and B. J. Georgeland, *Breakpoint and Beyond: Mastering the Future – Today*. HarperBusiness, 1992.

[19] D. Kelley and T. Kelley, 'Creative Confidence: Unleashing the Creative Potential Within Us All', 2013, doi: 10.48558/XSA6-0F24.

[20] 'What skills are becoming increasingly important for successful senior marketers?', Statista, 2022. Accessed: 1 December, 2022. [Online]. Available: https://www-statista-com.ezproxy.library.bi.no/statistics/659764/important-skills-marketers/

[21] R. Richards, 'Twelve potential benefits of living more creatively'. In *Everyday Creativity and the New Views of Human Nature*. American Psychological Association, 2007.

[22] M. J. C. Forgeard and J. C. Kaufman, 'Who Cares about Imagination, Creativity, and Innovation, and Why? A Review', *Psychol. Aesthet. Creat. Arts*, vol. 10, no. 3, pp. 250–269, August, 2016, doi: 10.1037/aca0000042.

[23] J. Hornberg and R. Reiter-Palmon, 'Creativity and the big five personality traits: is the relationship dependent on the creativity measure?' In *The Cambridge Handbook of Creativity and Personality Research (Cambridge Handbooks in Psychology)*, 1st ed., Cambridge University Press, 2017.

[24] G. J. Feist, R. Reiter-Palmon, and J. C. Kaufman, 'Introduction: the personal side of creativity: individual differences and the creative process'. In *The Cambridge Handbook of Creativity and Personality Research (Cambridge Handbooks in Psychology)*, 1st ed., Cambridge University Press, 2017.

[25] M. Černe, A. Carlsen, M. Škerlavaj, and A. Dysvik, 'Capitalizing on creativity: on enablers and barriers'. In *Capitalizing on Creativity at Work Fostering the Implementation of Creative Ideas in Organizations*, Edward Elgar Publishing, 2017.

[26] L. Sundararajan and J. R. Averill, 'Creativity in the everyday: culture, self and emotions'. In *Everyday Creativity and the New Views of Human Nature*, American Psychological Association, 2007.

[27] H. Raj and D. R. Saxena, 'Scientific Creativity: A Review of Researches', *Eur. Acad. Res.*, July, 2021. [Online]. Available: http://euacademic.org/UploadArticle/2494.pdf

[28] S. Kocabas, 'Element of Scientific Creivty', AAAI, Technical Report SS-93-1. Accessed: 2 October, 2022. [Online]. Available: www.aaai.org/Papers/Symposia/Spring/1993/SS-93-01/SS93-01-006.pdf

[29] R. Richards, 'Everyday creativity: our hidden potential.' In *Everyday Creativity and the New Views of Human Nature.* American Psychological Association, 2007.

[30] S. E. Woo, M. G. Keith, R. Su, R. Saef, and S. Parrigon, 'The curious dynamic between openness and interests in creativity.' In *The Cambridge Handbook of Creativity and Personality Research (Cambridge Handbooks in Psychology)*, 1st ed., Cambridge University Press, 2017.

[31] M. Diehl and W. Stroebe, 'Productivity Loss in Brainstorming Groups: Toward the Solution of a Riddle', *J. Pers. Soc. Psychol.*, vol. 53, no. 3, pp. 497–509, September, 1987, doi: 10.1037/0022-3514.53.3.497.

[32] H. H. Ransom, 'Victims of Groupthink: A Psychological Study of Foreign-Policy Decisions and Fiascoes. Irving L. Janis', *J. Polit.*, vol. 36, no. 1, pp. 218–220, February, 1974, doi: 10.2307/2129118.

[33] Z. Ivancevic and J. Hofmann, 'Emotions and creativity: from states to traits and emotion abilities.' In *The Cambridge Handbook of Creativity and Personality Research (Cambridge Handbooks in Psychology)*, 1st ed., Cambridge University Press, 2017.

[34] V. P. Glaveanu, 'Functional fixedness, creativity and problem-solving.' In *The Creativity Reader*, Oxford University Press, 2019.

[35] K. Duncker, 'On Problem Solving', *Psychological Monographs*, vol. 58(5) (Whole No. 270), 1945.

[36] T. Gruber, 'Great Apes Do Not Learn Novel Tool Use Easily: Conservatism, Functional Fixedness, or Cultural Influence?', *Int. J. Primatol.*, vol. 37, no. 2, pp. 296–316, April, 2016, doi: 10.1007/s10764-016-9902-4.

[37] F. Munoz-Rubke, D. Olson, R. Will, and K. H. James, 'Functional Fixedness in Tool Use: Learning Modality, Limitations and Individual Differences', *Acta Psychol. (Amst.)*, vol. 190, pp. 11–26, October, 2018, doi: 10.1016/j.actpsy.2018.06.006.

[38] D. Hanus, N. Mendes, C. Tennie, and J. Call, 'Comparing the Performances of Apes (Gorilla gorilla, Pan troglodytes, Pongo pygmaeus) and Human Children (Homo sapiens) in the Floating Peanut Task', *PLoS ONE*, vol. 6, no. 6, p. e19555, June, 2011, doi: 10.1371/journal.pone.0019555.

[39] M. A. Defeyter and T. P. German, 'Acquiring an Understanding of Design: Evidence from Children's Insight Problem Solving', *Cognition*, vol. 89, no. 2, pp. 133–155, September, 2003, doi: 10.1016/S0010-0277(03)00098-2.

[40] T. P. German and M. A. Defeyter, 'Immunity to Functional Fixedness in Young Children', *Psychon. Bull. Rev.*, vol. 7, no. 4, pp. 707–712, December, 2000, doi: 10.3758/BF03213010.

[41] T. T. U. Tran, R. Esseily, D. Bovet, and I. Király, 'One Function One Tool? A Review on Mutual Exclusivity in Tool Use Learning in Human and Non-human Species', *Front. Psychol.*, vol. 12, p. 603960, November, 2021, doi: 10.3389/fpsyg.2021.603960.

[42] E. G. Chrysikou, K. Motyka, C. Nigro, S.-I. Yang, and S. L. Thompson-Schill, 'Functional Fixedness in Creative Thinking Tasks Depends on Stimulus Modality', *Psychol. Aesthet. Creat. Arts*, vol. 10, no. 4, pp. 425–435, November, 2016, doi: 10.1037/aca0000050.

[43] M. Kroneisen, M. Kriechbaumer, S.-M. Kamp, and E. Erdfelder, 'How Can I Use It? The Role of Functional Fixedness in the Survival-processing Paradigm', *Psychon. Bull. Rev.*, vol. 28, no. 1, pp. 324–332, February, 2021, doi: 10.3758/s13423-020-01802-y.

[44] S. J. Ebel, D. Hanus, and J. Call, 'How Prior Experience and Task Presentation Modulate Innovation in 6-Year-Old-Children', *J. Exp. Child Psychol.*, vol. 180, pp. 87–103, April, 2019, doi: 10.1016/j.jecp.2018.12.004.

[45] A. Camarda *et al.*, 'Neural Basis of Functional Fixedness During Creative Idea Generation: An EEG Study', *Neuropsychologia*, vol. 118, pp. 4–12, September, 2018, doi: 10.1016/j.neuropsychologia.2018.03.009.

[46] E. G. Chrysikou and R. W. Weisberg, 'Following the Wrong Footsteps: Fixation Effects of Pictorial Examples in a Design Problem-Solving Task', *J. Exp. Psychol. Learn. Mem. Cogn.*, vol. 31, no. 5, pp. 1134–1148, 2005, doi: 10.1037/0278-7393.31.5.1134.

[47] 'The Late Show with Stephen Colbert', CBS, 30 October, 2015.

[48] A. Ledgerwood and A. E. Boydstun, 'Sticky Prospects: Loss Frames are Cognitively Stickier than Gain Frames', *J. Exp. Psychol. Gen.*, vol. 143, no. 1, pp. 376–385, February, 2014, doi: 10.1037/a0032310.

[49] T. McCaffrey, 'Innovation Relies on the Obscure: A Key to Overcoming the Classic Problem of Functional Fixedness', *Psychol. Sci.*, vol. 23, no. 3, pp. 215–218, March, 2012, doi: 10.1177/0956797611429580.

[50] B. W. Tuckman, 'Developmental Sequence in Small Groups', *Psychol. Bull.*, vol. 63, no. 6, pp. 384–399, June, 1965, doi: 10.1037/h0022100.

[51] 'The world's first deodorant designed for people with disabilities', Unilever. Accessed: 30 March, 2025. [Online]. Available: www.unilever.com/news/news-search/2021/the-worlds-first-deodorant-designed-for-people-with-disabilities/

[52] 'Clinical trials seek to fix their lack of racial mix', AAMC. Accessed: 18 February, 2025. [Online]. Available: www.aamc.org/news/clinical-trials-seek-fix-their-lack-racial-mix

[53] C. T. Tshetshema and K.-Y. Chan, 'A Systematic Literature Review of the Relationship Between Demographic Diversity and Innovation Performance at Team-level', *Technol. Anal. Strateg. Manag.*, vol. 32, no. 8, pp. 955–967, August, 2020, doi: 10.1080/09537325.2020.1730783.

[54] S. Huang, M. Battisti, and D. Pickernell, 'The Roles of Innovation Strategy and Founding Team Diversity in New Venture Growth', *J. Bus. Res.*, vol. 158, p. 113653, March, 2023, doi: 10.1016/j.jbusres.2023.113653.

[55] K. Kristinsson, M. Candi, and R. J. Sæmundsson, 'The Relationship between Founder Team Diversity and Innovation Performance: The Moderating Role of Causation Logic', *Long Range Plann.*, vol. 49, no. 4, pp. 464–476, August, 2016, doi: 10.1016/j.lrp.2015.12.013.

[56] J. Roh and J. Koo, 'The Impacts of Diversity on Team Innovation and the Moderating Effects of Cooperative Team Culture', *Int. Rev. Public Adm.*, vol. 24, no. 4, pp. 246–263, October, 2019, doi: 10.1080/12294659.2019.1688124.

[57] J. Han, S.-Q. Peng, C.-Y. CHIU, and A. K.-Y. LEUNG, 'Workforce Diversity and Creativity: A Multiple Level Model', Academy of International Business 49th Annual Meeting, 2007.

[58] J. M. Ruiz-Jiménez and M. D. M. Fuentes-Fuentes, 'Management Capabilities, Innovation, and Gender Diversity in the Top Management Team: An Empirical Analysis in Technology-based SMEs', *BRQ Bus. Res. Q.*, vol. 19, no. 2, pp. 107–121, April, 2016, doi: 10.1016/j.brq.2015.08.003.

[59] D. Van Knippenberg and M. C. Schippers, 'Work Group Diversity', *Annu. Rev. Psychol.*, vol. 58, no. 1, pp. 515–541, January, 2007, doi: 10.1146/annurev. psych.58.110405.085546.

[60] M. Weiss, J. Backmann, S. Razinskas, and M. Hoegl, 'Team Diversity in Innovation – Salient Research', *J. Prod. Innov. Manag.*, vol. 35, no. 5, pp. 839–850, September, 2018, doi: 10.1111/jpim.12465.

[61] 'Definition of Diversity'. Accessed: 18 February, 2025. [Online]. Available: www.merriam-webster.com/dictionary/diversity

[62] E. Velinov and M. Malý, 'Top Management Team Diversity and Company Performance: The moderating effect of Organization Life Cycle', *J. East. Eur. Cent. Asian Res. JEECAR*, vol. 3, no. 2, p. 11, December, 2016, doi: 10.15549/jeecar. v3i2.141.

[63] H. A. Krishnan and D. Park, 'A Few Good Women – On Top Management Teams', *J. Bus. Res.*, vol. 58, no. 12, pp. 1712–1720, December, 2005, doi: 10.1016/ j.jbusres.2004.09.003.

[64] 'Digest of Education Statistics'. Accessed: 18 February, 2025. [Online]. Available: https://nces.ed.gov/programs/digest/d23/tables/dt23_318.10.asp

[65] L. Z. Lindahl, 'Is This the Age of Women in Leadership?', Forbes. Accessed: 18 February, 2025. [Online]. Available: www.forbes.com/sites/lisalindahl/2024/ 02/05/is-this-the-age-of-women-in-leadership/

[66] General Medical Council, 'The state of medical education and practice in the UK, Workforce report', General Medical Council, 2024. [Online]. Available: www.gmc-uk.org/-/media/documents/somep-workforce-report-2024-full-report_ pdf-109169408.pdf

[67] 'Nation's physician workforce evolves: more women, a bit older, and toward different specialties', AAMC. Accessed: 18 February, 2025. [Online]. Available: www.aamc.org/news/nation-s-physician-workforce-evolves-more-women- bit-older-and-toward-different-specialties

[68] McKinsey & Company, 'Women in the Workplace 2024: The 10th-anniversary report', 2024. [Online]. Available: www.mckinsey.com/featured-insights/diversity-and-inclusion/women-in-the-workplace#/

[69] Y. Dai, G. Byun, and F. Ding, 'The Direct and Indirect Impact of Gender Diversity in New Venture Teams on Innovation Performance', *Entrep. Theory Pract.*, vol. 43, no. 3, pp. 505–528, May, 2019, doi: 10.1177/1042258718807696.

[70] McKinsey & Company, 'Diversity wins: How inclusion matters', 2020. [Online]. Available: www.mckinsey.com/featured-insights/diversity-and-inclusion/diversity-wins-how-inclusion-matters

[71] C. R. Østergaard, B. Timmermans, and K. Kristinsson, 'Does a Different View Create Something New? The Effect of Employee Diversity on Innovation', *Res. Policy*, vol. 40, no. 3, pp. 500–509, April, 2011, doi: 10.1016/j.respol.2010.11.004.

[72] M. Hemmert, C. K. Cho, and J. Y. Lee, 'Enhancing Innovation through Gender Diversity: A Two-country Study of Top Management Teams', *Eur. J. Innov. Manag.*, vol. 27, no. 1, pp. 193–213, January, 2024, doi: 10.1108/EJIM-08-2021-0383.

[73] C. Post, E. De Lia, N. DiTomaso, T. M. Tirpak, and R. Borwankar, 'Capitalizing on Thought Diversity for Innovation', *Res.-Technol. Manag.*, vol. 52, no. 6, pp. 14–25, November, 2009, doi: 10.1080/08956308.2009.11657596.

[74] W. Ruigrok, S. Peck, and S. Tacheva, 'Nationality and Gender Diversity on Swiss Corporate Boards', *Corp. Gov. Int. Rev.*, vol. 15, no. 4, pp. 546–557, July, 2007, doi: 10.1111/j.1467-8683.2007.00587.x.

[75] J. Fernández, 'The Impact of Gender Diversity in Foreign Subsidiaries' Innovation Outputs', *Int. J. Gend. Entrep.*, vol. 7, no. 2, pp. 148–167, January, 2015, doi: 10.1108/IJGE-07-2014-0022.

[76] 'Stillfront Group acquires Nanobit and expands the portfolio with narrative and lifestyle games', News Powered by Cision. Accessed: 18 April, 2025. [Online]. Available: https://news.cision.com/stillfront-group-ab/r/stillfront-group-acquires-nanobit-and-expands-the-portfolio-with-narrative-and-lifestyle-games,c3195937

[77] 'Novac – Alan Sumina: "Od naših 30 igara, najuspješnije su one koje ciljaju žensku populaciju."' Accessed: 18 April, 2025. [Online]. Available: https://novac.jutarnji.hr/novac/novi-svijet/alan-sumina-od-nasih-30-igara-najuspjesnije-su-one-koje-ciljaju-zensku-populaciju-9147332

[78] T. Yokoi, 'Female Gamers Are on the Rise. Can The Gaming Industry Catch Up?', Forbes. Accessed: 18 April, 2025. [Online]. Available: www.forbes.com/sites/tomokoyokoi/2021/03/04/female-gamers-are-on-the-rise-can-the-gaming-industry-catch-up/

[79] 'Gaming Market Size, Industry Share, Growth, Forecast, 2030.' Accessed: 18 April, 2025. [Online]. Available: www.fortunebusinessinsights.com/gaming-market-105730

[80] L. Xie, J. Zhou, Q. Zong, and Q. Lu, 'Gender Diversity in R&D Teams and Innovation Efficiency: Role of the Innovation Context', *Res. Policy*, vol. 49, no. 1, p. 103885, February, 2020, doi: 10.1016/j.respol.2019.103885.

[81] McKinsey & Company, 'Women in the Workplace', 2023. [Online]. Available: www.mckinsey.com/featured-insights/diversity-and-inclusion/women-in-the-workplace-2023#/

[82] A. H. Eagly and L. L. Carli, 'Women and the Labyrinth of Leadership', *Harv. Bus. Rev.*, vol. 85, no. 9, pp. 63–71, 2007.

[83] M. E. Heilman, 'Description and Prescription: How Gender Stereotypes Prevent Women's Ascent Up the Organizational Ladder', *J. Soc. Issues*, vol. 57, no. 4, pp. 657–674, January, 2001, doi: 10.1111/0022-4537.00234.

[84] H. Ibarra, 'A Lack of Sponsorship Is Keeping Women from Advancing into Leadership', *Harvard Business Review*, 19 August, 2019. Accessed: 11 April, 2025. [Online]. Available: https://hbr.org/2019/08/a-lack-of-sponsorship-is-keeping-women-from-advancing-into-leadership

[85] A. Krembs, 'How "sponsors" can achieve gender parity in leadership', *World Economic Forum*. [Online]. Available: www.weforum.org/stories/2023/11/sponsors-can-achieve-gender-parity-leadership/

[86] [Details known to the author], 'Source intentionally withheld due to anonymization.'

[87] 'Situasjonen for forskning i USA – og dermed hele verden – er dramatisk.' Accessed: 11 April, 2025. [Online]. Available: www.forskningsradet.no/forskningspolitikk-strategi/ltp/vi-mener/situasjonen-forskning-usa-er-dramatisk/

[88] N. Gallogly, 'Women Entrepreneurs Are Hitting a Funding Wall', *New York Times*, 21 September, 2024. [Online]. Available: www.nytimes.com/2024/09/21/business/women-entrepreneurs-are-hitting-a-funding-wall.html

[89] P. E. Vernon, *Creativity*. Penguin Education Psychology Readings, 1970.

[90] E. H. Schein and W. G. Bennis, *Personal and Organizational Change through Group Methods: The Laboratory Approach*, John Wiley & Sons Ltd, 1965.

[91] W. A. Kahn, 'Psychological Conditions of Personal Engagement and Disengagement at Work', *Acad. Manage. J.*, vol. 33, no. 4, pp. 692–724, 1990, doi: 10.2307/256287.

[92] A. Edmondson, 'Psychological Safety and Learning Behaviour in Work Teams', *Adm. Sci. Q.*, vol. 44, no. 2, pp. 350–383, 1999, doi: 10.2307/2666999.

[93] W. F. St. Amour, 'Interpersonal Risk Aversion: An Impediment to Learning and Knowledge Translation for Innovation', *Risk Manage.*, vol. 6, no. 2, pp. 31–47, 2004.

[94] A. Rapport, 'The Patient's Search for Safety: The Organizing Principle in Psychotherapy', *Psychotherapy*, vol. 34, no. 3, 1997. Accessed: 4 November, 2024. [Online]. Available: https://web.p.ebscohost.com/ehost/pdfviewer/pdfviewer?vid=0&sid=4b5facfa-0788-40c3-b138-c1f43aab73f7%40redis

[95] W. Swift and J. Copeland, 'Treatment Needs and Experiences of Australian Women with Alcohol and Other Drug Problems', *Drug Alcohol Depend.*, vol. 40, no. 3, pp. 211–219, March, 1996, doi: 10.1016/0376-8716(95)01209-5.

[96] S. Jha, 'Team Psychological Safety and Team Performance: A Moderated Mediation Analysis of Psychological Empowerment', *Int. J. Organ. Anal.*, vol. 27, no. 4, pp. 903–924, January, 2018, doi: 10.1108/IJOA-10-2018-1567.

[97] A. C. Edmondson, *The Fearless Organization: Creating Psychological Safety in the Workplace for Learning, Innovation, and Growth*. John Wiley & Sons, Inc, 2019.

[98] C. Argyris, 'Organizational Learning and Management Information Systems', *Account. Organ. Soc.*, vol. 2, no. 2, pp. 113–123, January, 1977, doi: 10.1016/0361-3682(77)90028-9.

[99] Google Re:work, 'Understand team effectiveness', Google Re:work. [Online]. Available: https://rework.withgoogle.com/en/guides/understanding-team-effectiveness#identify-dynamics-of-effective-teams

[100] S. Harvey, 'Creative Synthesis: Exploring the Process of Extraordinary Group Creativity', *Acad. Manage. Rev.*, vol. 39, no. 3, pp. 324–343, 2014.

[101] S. Harvey and C.-Y. Kou, 'Collective Engagement in Creative Tasks: The Role of Evaluation in the Creative Process in Groups', *Adm. Sci. Q.*, vol. 58, no. 3, pp. 346–386, September, 2013, doi: 10.1177/0001839213498591.

[102] A. Somech and A. Drach-Zahavy, 'Translating Team Creativity to Innovation Implementation: The Role of Team Composition and Climate for Innovation', *J. Manag.*, vol. 39, no. 3, pp. 684–708, March, 2013, doi: 10.1177/0149206310394187.

[103] J. Mukerjee and A. Metiu, 'Play and Psychological Safety: An Ethnography of Innovative Work', *J. Prod. Innov. Manag.*, vol. 39, no. 3, pp. 394–418, May, 2022, doi: 10.1111/jpim.12598.

[104] M. Andersson, O. Moen, and P. O. Brett, 'The Organizational Climate for Psychological Safety: Associations with SMEs' Innovation Capabilities and Innovation Performance', *J. Eng. Technol. Manag.*, vol. 55, p. 101554, January, 2020, doi: 10.1016/j.jengtecman.2020.101554.

[105] C. Sacramento, J. Lyubovnikova, I. Martinaityte, C. Gomes, L. Curral, and A. Juhasz-Wrench, 'Being Open, Feeling Safe and Getting Creative: The Role of Team Mean Openness to Experience in the Emergence of Team Psychological Safety and Team Creativity', *J. Prod. Innov. Manag.*, vol. 41, no. 1, pp. 12–35, January, 2024, doi: 10.1111/jpim.12699.

[106] H. Chesbrough, 'Business Model Innovation: Opportunities and Barriers', *Long Range Plann.*, vol. 43, no. 2–3, pp. 354–363, April, 2010, doi: 10.1016/j.lrp.2009.07.010.

[107] D. J. Teece, 'Business Models, Business Strategy and Innovation', *Long Range Plann.*, vol. 43, no. 2–3, pp. 172–194, April, 2010, doi: 10.1016/j.lrp.2009.07.003.

[108] Q. Miao, N. Eva, A. Newman, and B. Cooper, 'CEO Entrepreneurial Leadership and Performance Outcomes of Top Management Teams in Entrepreneurial Ventures: The Mediating Effects of Psychological Safety', *J. Small Bus. Manag.*, vol. 57, no. 3, pp. 1119–1135, July, 2019, doi: 10.1111/jsbm.12465.

[109] P. Agarwal and E. Farndale, 'High-performance Work Systems and Creativity Implementation: The Role of Psychological Capital and Psychological Safety', *Hum. Resour. Manag. J.*, vol. 27, no. 3, pp. 440–458, July, 2017, doi: 10.1111/1748-8583.12148.

[110] C. Peterson, 'The Future of Optimism', *Am. Psychol.*, vol. 55, no. 1, pp. 44–55, January, 2000, doi: 10.1037/0003-066X.55.1.44.

[111] S. P. Brown and T. W. Leigh, 'A New Look at Psychological Climate and its Relationship to Job Involvement, Effort, and Performance', *J. Appl. Psychol.*, vol. 81, no. 4, pp. 358–368, August, 1996, doi: 10.1037/0021-9010.81.4.358.

[112] R. Kark and A. Carmeli, 'Alive and Creating: The Mediating Role of Vitality and Aliveness in the Relationship between Psychological Safety and Creative Work Involvement', *J. Organ. Behav.*, vol. 30, no. 6, pp. 785–804, August, 2009, doi: 10.1002/job.571.

[113] M. L. Frazier, S. Fainshmidt, R. L. Klinger, A. Pezeshkan, and V. Vracheva, 'Psychological Safety: A Meta-Analytic Review and Extension', *Pers. Psychol.*, vol. 70, no. 1, pp. 113–165, February, 2017, doi: 10.1111/peps.12183.

[114] B. Schneider and A. E. Reichers, 'On the Etiology of Climates', *Pers. Psychol.*, vol. 36, no. 1, pp. 19–39, March, 1983, doi: 10.1111/j.1744-6570.1983.tb00500.x.

[115] J. Koopmann, K. Lanaj, M. Wang, L. Zhou, and J. Shi, 'Nonlinear Effects of Team Tenure on Team Psychological Safety Climate and Climate Strength: Implications for Average Team Member Performance', *J. Appl. Psychol.*, vol. 101, no. 7, pp. 940–957, July, 2016, doi: 10.1037/apl0000097.

[116] H. Peng and F. Wei, 'How and When Does Leader Behavioural Integrity Influence Employee Voice? The Roles of Team Independence Climate and Corporate Ethical Values', *J. Bus. Ethics*, vol. 166, no. 3, pp. 505–521, October, 2020, doi: 10.1007/s10551-019-04114-x.

[117] G. Wang, J. Li, H. Liu, and C. Zaggia, 'Transformational Leadership and Teachers' Voice Behaviour: A Moderated Mediation Model of Group Voice Climate and Team Psychological Safety', *Educ. Manag. Adm. Leadersh.*, p. 174114322211434, February, 2023, doi: 10.1177/17411432221143452.

[118] C. G. V. Coutifaris and A. M. Grant, 'Taking Your Team Behind the Curtain: The Effects of Leader Feedback-Sharing and Feedback-Seeking on Team Psychological Safety', *Organ. Sci.*, vol. 33, no. 4, pp. 1574–1598, July, 2022, doi: 10.1287/orsc.2021.1498.

[119] K. W. Thomas and B. A. Velthouse, 'Cognitive Elements of Empowerment: An "Interpretive" Model of Intrinsic Task Motivation', *Acad. Manage. Rev.*, vol. 15, no. 4, pp. 666–681, October, 1990, doi: 10.5465/amr.1990.4310926.

[120] A. W. Brooks, K. Huang, N. Abi-Esber, R. W. Buell, L. Huang, and B. Hall, 'Mitigating Malicious Envy: Why Successful Individuals Should Reveal their Failures', *J. Exp. Psychol. Gen.*, vol. 148, no. 4, pp. 667–687, April, 2019, doi: 10.1037/xge0000538.

[121] B. P. Owens and D. R. Hekman, 'How Does Leader Humility Influence Team Performance? Exploring the Mechanisms of Contagion and Collective Promotion Focus', *Acad. Manage. J.*, vol. 59, no. 3, pp. 1088–1111, June, 2016, doi: 10.5465/amj.2013.0660.

[122] J. Hu, B. Erdogan, K. Jiang, T. N. Bauer, and S. Liu, 'Leader Humility and Team Creativity: The Role of Team Information Sharing, Psychological Safety, and Power Distance', *J. Appl. Psychol.*, vol. 103, no. 3, pp. 313–323, March, 2018, doi: 10.1037/apl0000277.

[123] B. L. Kirkman and B. Rosen, 'Beyond Self-Management: Antecedents and Consequences of Team Empowerment', *Acad. Manage. J.*, vol. 42, no. 1, pp. 58–74, February, 1999, doi: 10.2307/256874.

[124] M. Ahearne, J. Mathieu, and A. Rapp, 'To Empower or Not to Empower Your Sales Force? An Empirical Examination of the Influence of Leadership Empowerment Behaviour on Customer Satisfaction and Performance', *J. Appl. Psychol.*, vol. 90, no. 5, pp. 945–955, 2005, doi: 10.1037/0021-9010.90.5.945.

[125] J. Zhu, J. Yao, and L. Zhang, 'Linking Empowering Leadership to Innovative Behaviour in Professional Learning Communities: The Role of Psychological Empowerment and Team Psychological Safety', *Asia Pac. Educ. Rev.*, vol. 20, no. 4, pp. 657–671, December 2019, doi: 10.1007/s12564-019-09584-2.

[126] H. Leroy et al., 'Behavioural Integrity for Safety, Priority of Safety, Psychological Safety, and Patient Safety: A Team-level Study', *J. Appl. Psychol.*, vol. 97, no. 6, pp. 1273–1281, 2012, doi: 10.1037/a0030076.

[127] T. Simons, *The Integrity Dividend: Leading by the Power of Your Word*. Jossey-Bass, 2008.

[128] D. M. Rousseau, S. B. Sitkin, R. S. Burt, and C. Camerer, 'Introduction to Special Topic Forum: Not so Different after All: A Cross-Discipline View of Trust', *Acad. Manage. Rev.*, vol. 23, no. 3, pp. 393–404, 1998.

[129] Z. Xu, J. Gong, Y. Qu, and X. Sun, 'Using Leader Affiliative Humour to Encourage Employee Knowledge Sharing: The Multilevel Role of Knowledge Sharing Self-efficacy and Team Psychological Safety', *J. Innov. Knowl.*, vol. 8, no. 3, p. 100408, July, 2023, doi: 10.1016/j.jik.2023.100408.

[130] S. Fayyad, 'The Role of Employee Trust in the Relationship Between Leaders' Aggressive Humour and Knowledge Sharing', *J. Assoc. Arab Univ. Tour. Hosp.*, vol. 19, no. 1, pp. 143–157, December, 2020, doi: 10.21608/jaauth.2020.45371.1079.

[131] L. L. Martins, M. C. Schilpzand, B. L. Kirkman, S. Ivanaj, and V. Ivanaj, 'A Contingency View of the Effects of Cognitive Diversity on Team Performance: The Moderating Roles of Team Psychological Safety and Relationship Conflict', *Small Group Res.*, vol. 44, no. 2, pp. 96–126, April, 2013, doi: 10.1177/1046496412466921.

[132] S. J. Shin and J. Zhou, 'When is educational Specialization Heterogeneity Related to Creativity in Research and Development Teams? Transformational Leadership as a Moderator', *J. Appl. Psychol.*, vol. 92, no. 6, pp. 1709–1721, November, 2007, doi: 10.1037/0021-9010.92.6.1709.

[133] C. Smythe and P. Hurtado, 'Volkswagen Probed by States Over Pollution Cheating', Bloomberg.com. [Online]. Available: www.bloomberg.com/news/articles/2015-09-22/volkswagen-probed-by-u-s-multistate-group-on-pollution-cheating?embedded-checkout=true

[134] A. Chandrasekaran and A. Mishra, 'Task Design, Team Context, and Psychological Safety: An Empirical Analysis of R&D Projects in High Technology

Organizations', *Prod. Oper. Manag.*, vol. 21, no. 6, pp. 977–996, November, 2012, doi: 10.1111/j.1937-5956.2012.01329.x.

[135] E. N. Sherf, M. R. Parke, and S. Isaakyan, 'Distinguishing Voice and Silence at Work: Unique Relationships with Perceived Impact, Psychological Safety, and Burnout', *Acad. Manage. J.*, vol. 64, no. 1, pp. 114–148, February, 2021, doi: 10.5465/amj.2018.1428.

[136] K. Sjöblom, J.-P. Mäkiniemi, and A. Mäkikangas, '"I Was Given Three Marks and Told to Buy a Porsche" – Supervisors' Experiences of Leading Psychosocial Safety Climate and Team Psychological Safety in a Remote Academic Setting', *Int. J. Environ. Res. Public. Health*, vol. 19, no. 19, p. 12016, September, 2022, doi: 10.3390/ijerph191912016.

[137] Y. Liu and R. T. Keller, 'How Psychological Safety Impacts R&D Project Teams' Performance', *Res.-Technol. Manag.*, vol. 64, no. 2, pp. 39–45, March, 2021, doi: 10.1080/08956308.2021.1863111.

[138] M. S. Mehmood, Z. Jian, U. Akram, Z. Akram, and Y. Tanveer, 'Entrepreneurial Leadership and Team Creativity: The Roles of Team Psychological Safety and Knowledge Sharing', *Pers. Rev.*, vol. 51, no. 9, pp. 2404–2425, December, 2022, doi: 10.1108/PR-07-2020-0517.

[139] C. J. Roussin, T. L. MacLean, and J. W. Rudolph, 'The Safety in Unsafe Teams: A Multilevel Approach to Team Psychological Safety', *J. Manag.*, vol. 42, no. 6, pp. 1409–1433, September, 2016, doi: 10.1177/0149206314525204.

[140] J. R. Pierce and H. Aguinis, 'The Too-Much-of-a-Good-Thing Effect in Management', *J. Manag.*, vol. 39, no. 2, pp. 313–338, February, 2013, doi: 10.1177/0149206311410060.

[141] T. Budianto, E. Susanto, S. Sitalaksmi, and G. Kismono, 'Team Monitoring, Does it Matter for Team Performance? Moderating role of Team Monitoring on Team Psychological Safety and Team Learning', *J. Indones. Econ. Bus.*, vol. 35, no. 2, p. 81, May, 2020, doi: 10.22146/jieb.54522.

[142] '6 Reasons Why Nokia Failed?', StartupTalky. Accessed: 19 February, 2025. [Online]. Available: https://startuptalky.com/reasons-why-nokia-failed/

[143] 'EU faces major barriers to deploying artificial intelligence | Science|Business.' Accessed: 11 April, 2025. [Online]. Available: https://sciencebusiness.net/news/european-institute-innovation-and-technology/eu-faces-major-barriers-deploying-artificial

[144] P. Koellinger, 'The Relationship between Technology, Innovation, and Firm Performance – Empirical Evidence from E-business in Europe', *Res. Policy*, vol. 37, no. 8, pp. 1317–1328, September, 2008, doi: 10.1016/j.respol.2008.04.024.

[145] OECD, *OECD Digital Economy Outlook 2024 (Volume 1): Embracing the Technology Frontier*. In OECD Digital Economy Outlook. OECD, 2024, doi: 10.1787/a1689dc5-en.

[146] M. A. Trabelsi, 'The Impact of Artificial Intelligence on Economic Development', *J. Electron. Bus. Digit. Econ.*, vol. 3, no. 2, pp. 142–155, January, 2024, doi: 10.1108/JEBDE-10-2023-0022.

[147] 'Harnessing Artificial Intelligence in Drug Discovery and Development.' Accessed: 15 February, 2025. [Online]. Available: www.accc-cancer.org/acccbuzz/blog-post-template/accc-buzz/2024/12/20/harnessing-artificial-intelligence-in-drug-discovery-and-development

[148] J. Åström, W. Reim, and V. Parida, 'Value Creation and Value Capture for AI Business Model Innovation: A Three-phase Process Framework', *Rev. Manag. Sci.*, vol. 16, no. 7, pp. 2111–2133, October, 2022, doi: 10.1007/s11846-022-00521-z.

[149] G. Vial, 'Understanding Digital Transformation: A Review and a Research Agenda', *J. Strateg. Inf. Syst.*, vol. 28, no. 2, pp. 118–144, June, 2019, doi: 10.1016/j.jsis.2019.01.003.

[150] V. Parida, D. Sjödin, and W. Reim, 'Reviewing Literature on Digitalization, Business Model Innovation, and Sustainable Industry: Past Achievements and Future Promises', *Sustainability*, vol. 11, no. 2, p. 391, January, 2019, doi: 10.3390/su11020391.

[151] K. Talke and S. Heidenreich, 'How to Overcome Pro-Change Bias: Incorporating Passive and Active Innovation Resistance in Innovation Decision Models', *J. Prod. Innov. Manag.*, vol. 31, no. 5, pp. 894–907, September, 2014, doi: 10.1111/jpim.12130.

[152] S. Oreg, 'Resistance to Change: Developing an Individual Differences Measure', *J. Appl. Psychol.*, vol. 88, no. 4, pp. 680–693, 2003, doi: 10.1037/0021-9010.88.4.680.

[153] A. Raj, J. A. Kumar, and P. Bansal, 'A Multicriteria Decision Making Approach to Study Barriers to the Adoption of Autonomous Vehicles', *Transp. Res. Part Policy Pract.*, vol. 133, pp. 122–137, March, 2020, doi: 10.1016/j.tra.2020.01.013.

[154] J. Hudson, M. Orviska, and J. Hunady, 'People's Attitudes to Autonomous Vehicles', *Transp. Res. Part Policy Pract.*, vol. 121, pp. 164–176, March, 2019, doi: 10.1016/j.tra.2018.08.018.

[155] E. M. Rogers, *Diffusion of innovations*, 3rd ed. The Free Press, 1971.

[156] D. C. Hambrick and P. A. Mason, 'Upper Echelons: The Organization as a Reflection of Its Top Managers', *Acad. Manage. Rev.*, vol. 9, no. 2, p. 193, April, 1984, doi: 10.2307/258434.

[157] C. Kurzhals, L. Graf-Vlachy, and A. König, 'Strategic Leadership and Technological Innovation: A Comprehensive Review and Research Agenda', *Corp. Gov. Int. Rev.*, vol. 28, no. 6, pp. 437–464, November, 2020, doi: 10.1111/corg.12351.

[158] A. Madanaguli, V. Parida, P. Oghazi, and P. K. Tran, 'Technological Innovation Adoption Among Swedish Healthcare Professionals: A Contingency Technology Adoption Framework', *IEEE Trans. Eng. Manag.*, vol. 71, pp. 13006–13019, 2024, doi: 10.1109/TEM.2023.3327597.

[159] S. Nadella and J. Euchner, 'Navigating Digital Transformation: An Interview with Satya Nadella', *Res.-Technol. Manag.*, vol. 61, no. 4, pp. 11–15, July, 2018, doi: 10.1080/08956308.2018.1471272.

[160] J. Füller, K. Hutter, J. Wahl, V. Bilgram, and Z. Tekic, 'How AI Revolutionizes Innovation Management: Perceptions and Implementation Preferences of AI-based Innovators', *Technol. Forecast. Soc. Change*, vol. 178, p. 121598, May, 2022, doi: 10.1016/j.techfore.2022.121598.

[161] United Nations, 'The Digital Economy Report 2024, Shaping an environmentally sustainable and inclusive digital future', United Nations Publications, 978-92-1-358977–9, 2024. Accessed: 25 August, 2024. [Online]. Available: https://unctad.org/system/files/official-document/der2024_en.pdf

[162] 'Netflix model for antibiotic subscriptions | LSHTM.' Accessed: 21 April, 2025. [Online]. Available: www.lshtm.ac.uk/research/centres/amr/news/426171/netflix-model-antibiotic-subscriptions

[163] S. Sundland, 'Case Study: Sparebanken Vest Building Culture, Technology, and Trust Together', 14 April, 2025.

[164] United Nations, 'Sustainability', www.un.org/. Accessed: 1 September, 2024. [Online]. Available: www.un.org/en/academic-impact/sustainability

[165] S. Zhou, Md. H. U. Rashid, S. A. Mohd. Zobair, F. A. Sobhani, and A. B. Siddik, 'Does ESG Impact Firms' Sustainability Performance? The Mediating Effect of Innovation Performance', *Sustainability*, vol. 15, no. 6, p. 5586, March, 2023, doi: 10.3390/su15065586.

[166] 'CB Insights – Your all-in-one AI super analyst', CB Insights. Accessed: 17 February, 2025. [Online]. Available: www.cbinsights.com/

[167] D. Hu, Y. Wang, J. Huang, and H. Huang, 'How do different Innovation Forms Mediate the Relationship between Environmental Regulation and Performance?', *J. Clean. Prod.*, vol. 161, pp. 466–476, September, 2017, doi: 10.1016/j.jclepro.2017.05.152.

[168] M. E. Porter, 'Essay', *Sci. Am.*, vol. 264, no. 4, pp. 168–168, April, 1991, doi: 10.1038/scientificamerican0491-168.

[169] M. E. Porter and C. V. D. Linde, 'Toward a New Conception of the Environment-Competitiveness Relationship', *J. Econ. Perspect.*, vol. 9, no. 4, pp. 97–118, November, 1995, doi: 10.1257/jep.9.4.97.

[170] Y. Rubashkina, M. Galeotti, and E. Verdolini, 'Environmental Regulation and Competitiveness: Empirical Evidence on the Porter Hypothesis from European Manufacturing Sectors', *Energy Policy*, vol. 83, pp. 288–300, August, 2015, doi: 10.1016/j.enpol.2015.02.014.

[171] N. Johnstone, S. Managi, M. C. Rodríguez, I. Haščič, H. Fujii, and M. Souchier, 'Environmental Policy Design, Innovation and Efficiency Gains in Electricity Generation', *Energy Econ.*, vol. 63, pp. 106–115, March, 2017, doi: 10.1016/j.eneco.2017.01.014.

[172] M. Bu, Z. Qiao, and B. Liu, 'Voluntary Environmental Regulation and Firm Innovation in China', *Econ. Model.*, vol. 89, pp. 10–18, July, 2020, doi: 10.1016/j.econmod.2019.12.020.

[173] R. Gonçalves, B. Vlačić, M. González-Loureiro, and R. Sousa, 'The Impact of Open Innovation on the Environmental Sustainability Practices and International Sales Intensity Nexus: A Multicountry Study', *Int. Bus. Rev.*, vol. 33, no. 5, p. 102279, October, 2024, doi: 10.1016/j.ibusrev.2024.102279.

[174] P. K. Dey, C. Malesios, D. De, S. Chowdhury, and F. B. Abdelaziz, 'The Impact of Lean Management Practices and Sustainably-Oriented Innovation on Sustainability Performance of Small and Medium-Sized Enterprises: Empirical Evidence from the UK', *Br. J. Manag.*, vol. 31, no. 1, pp. 141–161, January, 2020, doi: 10.1111/1467-8551.12388.

[175] R. Masocha, 'Does Environmental Sustainability Impact Innovation, Ecological and Social Measures of Firm Performance of SMEs? Evidence from South Africa', *Sustainability*, vol. 10, no. 11, p. 3855, October, 2018, doi: 10.3390/su10113855.

[176] K. Kajtazi, G. Rexhepi, A. Sharif, and I. Ozturk, 'Business Model Innovation and its Impact on Corporate Sustainability', *J. Bus. Res.*, vol. 166, p. 114082, November, 2023, doi: 10.1016/j.jbusres.2023.114082.

[177] A. B. Jaffe and K. Palmer, 'Environmental Regulation and Innovation: A Panel Data Study', *Rev. Econ. Stat.*, vol. 79, no. 4, pp. 610–619, November, 1997, doi: 10.1162/003465397557196.

[178] European Commission, 'Corporate sustainability reporting', https://finance.ec.europa.eu/. Accessed: 10 September, 2024. [Online]. Available: https://finance.ec.europa.eu/capital-markets-union-and-financial-markets/company-reporting-and-auditing/company-reporting/corporate-sustainability-reporting_en

[179] S. E. A. Dixon and A. Clifford, 'Ecopreneurship: A New Approach to Managing the Triple Bottom Line', *J. Organ. Change Manag.*, vol. 20, no. 3, pp. 326–345, May, 2007, doi: 10.1108/09534810710740164.

[180] L. Fagan, 'Virtual meetings have power to lower carbon emissions', www.sustainability-times.com/. Accessed: 7 September, 2024. [Online]. Available: www.sustainability-times.com/sustainable-business/virtual-meetings-have-power-to-lower-carbon-emissions/

[181] Z. Forian, 'Owning a Car is Less Important to Younger Generations', Statista.com. Accessed: 15 November, 2024. [Online]. Available: www.statista.com/chart/33097/importance-of-owning-a-car-for-us-residents-by-generation/

[182] R. Bohne, 'Value of the sharing economy worldwide in 2021 and 2023 with a forecast for 2027 and 2031', Statista.com. Accessed: 15 November, 2024. [Online]. Available: www.statista.com/statistics/830986/value-of-the-global-sharing-economy/

[183] 'Right to repair: Making repair easier and more appealing to consumers | News | European Parliament'. Accessed: 17 February, 2025. [Online]. Available:

www.europarl.europa.eu/news/en/press-room/20240419IPR20590/right-to-repair-making-repair-easier-and-more-appealing-to-consumers

[184] S. Jørgensen and L. J. T. Pedersen, 'RESTART Sustainable Business Model Innovation.' In *Palgrave Studies in Sustainable Business in Association with Future Earth*. Springer International Publishing, 2018, doi: 10.1007/978-3-319-91971-3.

[185] 'IKEA Buy back & resell – Sustainable furniture.' Accessed: 17 February, 2025. [Online]. Available: www.ikea.com/us/en/customer-service/services/buy-back/

[186] C. Villamil and S. Hallstedt, 'Sustainability Integration in Product Portfolio for Sustainable Development: Findings from the Industry', *Bus. Strategy Environ.*, vol. 30, no. 1, pp. 388–403, January, 2021, doi: 10.1002/bse.2627.

[187] D. Töbelmann and T. Wendler, 'The Impact of Environmental Innovation on Carbon Dioxide Emissions', *J. Clean. Prod.*, vol. 244, p. 118787, January, 2020, doi: 10.1016/j.jclepro.2019.118787.

[188] C. Cheng *et al.*, 'Impact of Green Process Innovation and Productivity on Sustainability: The Moderating Role of Environmental Awareness', *Sustainability*, vol. 15, no. 17, p. 12945, August, 2023, doi: 10.3390/su151712945.

[189] 'Dette er BIR – BIR.' Accessed: 30 March, 2025. [Online]. Available: https://bir.no/om-bir/om-konsernet/

[190] A. T. Pedersen, 'Case Study: BIR AS – Pioneering Sustainable Innovation in Waste Management', 24 February, 2025.

[191] *The Economist*, 'An Eco-wakening – Measuring global awareness, engagement and action for nature', The Economist Intelligence Unit, 2021. [Online]. Available: https://f.hubspotusercontent20.net/hubfs/4783129/An%20EcoWakening_Measuring%20awareness,%20engagement%20and%20action%20for%20nature_FINAL_MAY%202021%20(1).pdf?__hstc=130722960.ecb206528da823f5ba86141aa6e8eac6.1642377481532.1642377481532.1642377481532.1&__hssc=130722960.1.1642377481533&__hsfp=2719519617&hsCtaTracking=96a022a5-8be1-44ee-82fc-ced6164b8590%7C0c8892b7-4e13-464f-9b50-75e692c189ef

[192] McKinsey & Co, 'The State of Fashion 2020', 2020. [Online]. Available: www.mckinsey.com/~/media/mckinsey/industries/retail/our%20insights/the%20state%20of%20fashion%202020%20navigating%20uncertainty/the-state-of-fashion-2020-final.pdf

[193] Accenture, 'More than Half of Consumers Would Pay More for Sustainable Products Designed to Be Reused or Recycled, Accenture Survey Finds', newsroom.accenture.com. Accessed: 9 September, 2024. [Online]. Available: https://newsroom.accenture.com/news/2019/more-than-half-of-consumers-would-pay-more-for-sustainable-products-designed-to-be-reused-or-recycled-accenture-survey-finds

[194] 'New Kroll Study Shows Stronger Investment Returns for Companies with High ESG Ratings', *Kroll*. Accessed: 17 February, 2025. [Online]. Available: www.kroll.com/en/about-us/news/kroll-study-shows-stronger-investment-returns-companies-high-esg-ratings

[195] A. Reichheld, J. Peto, and C. Ritthaler, 'Research: Consumers' Sustainability Demands Are Rising', *HBR*, 18 September, 2023. [Online]. Available: https://hbr.org/2023/09/research-consumers-sustainability-demands-are-rising

[196] C. Camisón-Zornoza, R. Lapiedra-Alcamí, M. Segarra-Ciprés, and M. Boronat-Navarro, 'A Meta-analysis of Innovation and Organizational Size', *Organ. Stud.*, vol. 25, no. 3, pp. 331–361, March, 2004, doi: 10.1177/0170840604040039.

[197] K. Jaskyte, 'Does Size Really Matter? Organizational Size and Innovations in Nonprofit Organizations', *Nonprofit Manag. Leadersh.*, vol. 24, no. 2, pp. 229–247, December, 2013, doi: 10.1002/nml.21087.

[198] C. Camarero, M. J. Garrido, and E. Vicente, 'How Cultural Organizations' Size and Funding Influence Innovation and Performance: The Case of Museums', *J. Cult. Econ.*, vol. 35, no. 4, pp. 247–266, November, 2011, doi: 10.1007/s10824-011-9144-4.

[199] C. S. Jung and G. Lee, 'Organizational Climate, Leadership, Organization Size, and Aspiration for Innovation in Government Agencies', *Public Perform. Manag. Rev.*, vol. 39, no. 4, pp. 757–782, June, 2016, doi: 10.1080/15309576.2015.1137764.

[200] OECD, 'OECD Science, Technology and Industry Outlook 2012'. In *OECD Science, Technology and Industry Outlook*, OECD, 2012, doi: 10.1787/sti_outlook-2012-en.

[201] A. M. Knott and C. Vieregger, 'Reconciling the Firm Size and Innovation Puzzle', *Organ. Sci.*, vol. 31, no. 2, pp. 477–488, March, 2020, doi: 10.1287/orsc.2019.1310.

[202] M. Fritsch and M. Meschede, 'Product Innovation, Process Innovation and Size', *Rev. Ind. Organ.*, no. 19, 2001.

[203] H. Lim and C. Han, 'National Borders Transcended: The Impact of Geographical Proximity on the Growth of Global Innovation Networks among Cities in East Asia', *Int. J. Urban Sci.*, vol. 27, no. 4, pp. 570–598, October, 2023, doi: 10.1080/12265934.2021.1915854.

[204] S. Rastvortseva and A. Amanalieva, 'The Concept of Technological Proximity in the Development of European Union National Innovative Systems', *Bull. Geogr. Socio-Econ. Ser.*, no. 51, pp. 35–46, March, 2021, doi: 10.2478/bog-2021-0003.

[205] W. Hölzl and J. Janger, 'Distance to the Frontier and the Perception of Innovation Barriers across European Countries', *Res. Policy*, vol. 43, no. 4, pp. 707–725, May, 2014, doi: 10.1016/j.respol.2013.10.001.

[206] D. Archibugi, A. Filippetti, and M. Frenz, 'Economic Crisis and Innovation: Is Destruction Prevailing over Accumulation?', *Res. Policy*, vol. 42, no. 2, pp. 303–314, March, 2013, doi: 10.1016/j.respol.2012.07.002.

[207] A. Filippetti and D. Archibugi, 'Innovation in Times of Crisis: National Systems of Innovation, Structure, and Demand', *Res. Policy*, vol. 40, no. 2, pp. 179–192, March, 2011, doi: 10.1016/j.respol.2010.09.001.

[208] 'A Simple Tool You Need to Manage Innovation', *Harvard Business Review*, 31 May, 2012. Accessed: 23 February, 2025. [Online]. Available: https://hbr.org/2012/05/a-simple-tool-you-need-to-mana

[209] D. Hillson, 'Towards a Risk Maturity Model', *Int. J. Proj. Bus. Risk Manag.*, 1997.

Index